Building Your Swing for Better Golf with Amy Alcott

Building Your Swing for Better Golf with Amy Alcott

Maxine Van Evera

Illustrations by Jan Nichols
Consultant illustrator: Dom Lupo

SAN DIEGO • NEW YORK
A. S. BARNES & COMPANY, INC.
IN LONDON:
THE TANTIVY PRESS

First Edition
Manufactured in the United States of America

For information write to:
A.S. Barnes & Company, Inc.
P.O. Box 3051
La Jolla, California 92038

The Tantivy Press
Magdalen House
136-148 Tooley Street
London, SE1 2TT, England

Library of Congress Cataloging in Publication Data

Van Evera, Maxine, 1921-
    Building your swing for better golf with Amy Alcott.

    Includes index.
    1. Swing (Golf)   I. Alcott, Amy.   II. Title.
GV 979.S9V36   796.352'3   78-69645
ISBN 0-498-02141-6

    2 3 4 5 6 7 8 9   84 83 82

Contents

Foreword

To my friends, fellow golfers, and all golf enthusiasts:

I am pleased to affiliate myself with this fine book on golf technique. Many books have been written on golf instruction, but I feel *Building Your Swing for Better Golf* has special merit in that it affords the interested golfer an opportunity to study and enhance his or her knowledge of the basic golf swing.

Maxine Van Evera has written a book which might be termed a golf handbook on basic fundamentals, but the connotation of the word "handbook" does not really define the quality of this golf book. The building process presented throughout is an innovative method that golfers may use to help them understand the basic swing. Once the basic swing is clear, they can better understand their own golf swings—which is a key to self-improvement. Hitting a golf ball is one thing, but improving one's game and developing consistency in hitting the ball with positive repetition comes only through practicing good fundamentals. Like most professionals, I believe fundamentals to be the building block for the swing.

As a golf professional, I endorse this book as an excellent study guide. The book is for the beginner or pro, Sunday golfer or golf purist. It is for anyone who may want to enrich his or her knowledge of the basic golf swing in order to improve his or her own golf swing.

It has been said time and time again that golf is an individual game; that everyone swings differently. This is true. Even though my own golf swing deviates from the basic swing presented in the book, I find the basic "keys" that have been developed work by basing my swing on these same fundamentals. Although everyone may swing differently, my feeling is that each person can swing more effectively by developing basic keys—based on fundamentals—that work especially for them. Let this be your goal then while studying the basic swing: rather than searching for perfection by exact duplication of the basic golf swing, use the basic swing for guidelines and search for simple keys to make your own swing better. With determination, practice, and patience you will gain greater enjoyment from this, the greatest game of 'em all, through *Building Your Swing for Better Golf.*

Good golfing and happy days,
Amy Alcott

Acknowledgments

My sincere appreciation is extended to friends, students, and associates whose personal encouragement provided continuing enthusiasm for the writing of this book. Special appreciation is given to the late Dick Chapman, Dr. Raymond Snyder, and PGA professionals Eddie Merrins, John Ruedi, and Fred Sherman—each of whom knew or knows his personal contribution. Appreciation is also extended to Anne Miller, whose photographs of Amy Alcott appear throughout the book, and to Jan Nichols and consulting artist Dom Lupo for providing illustrations.

Although special appreciation for help and encouragement is given to those who are mentioned (and to many who are not), my indebtedness is to my family and my long-suffering friends, whose patience and endurance helped all of us survive the completion of the book.

Maxine Van Evera

Building Your Swing for Better Golf with Amy Alcott

1

Why Build the Swing?

The golf swing is a combination of many separate, interrelated, moving parts of the body which each work independently yet together to achieve the whole. Although independent actions within the golf swing are all fairly natural, problems in golf occur because the golf swing itself, as a single action, is not a natural movement. A natural swing develops, however, by learning how to establish and swing through positions that promote coordination peculiar only to golf.

Unlike many sports that combine a naturally coordinated swinging movement of arms and legs to attain specific skills—such as in tennis or baseball—the golf swing calls for an unnatural coordination of muscles. In golf the body turns rotationally while the arms swing upright together; movements which are natural in themselves but unnatural when combined to negotiate the swing required in golf. *Natural* movements of the body—outside of golf—seldom require this same coordination. Consequently, learning or improving in golf makes it necessary to help these movements coordinate by establishing positions that enable them to do so.

The time-proven basic golf swing has evolved as a series of related fundamental positions that promote coordination and fundamental movements that smooth positions together for a coordinated swing. The dictionary defines a fundamental as: "a principle, rule, law, etc., that forms a foundation or basis; essential part; indispensable, underlying." As applied to golf, the definition defines a golf fundamental as an essential position or movement that is indispensable in building a strong foundation for the swing. This stresses the importance of applying fundamentals to establish positions that promote coordination. It cannot be disputed that using fundamentals to establish accurate positions is the best approach to a sound, repeating, swing; but, unfortunately, only a handful among thousands of golfers either understand or apply the principles involved.

Building the swing is not for the purpose of abolishing old golf swings in favor of standardized new ones. Golf is a personal thing and it is neither realistic nor expected that golfers should start all over again and build a new golf swing. All golfers use some fundamentals whether they are aware of it or not. And while they may use some fundamentals unknowingly, the fact is that most golf swings can be improved upon or corrected by learning to use *more* fundamentals with greater effectiveness. Because of the number of fundamentals which make up the swing, however, golfers seldom use or exclude the same ones; consequently, all golf swings are not improved upon or corrected by using the same fundamentals. Learning which fundamentals affect each individual swing is the key to self-improvement.

Understanding the golf swing by building the *basic* swing will enable golfers to correct or adjust those parts of their own golf swing that are not fundamentally correct by comparing their swing with the basic swing. In that way they can improve personal performance and proficiency by learning how to establish positions initially that promote coordination while developing a capability for analyzing and correcting swing defects.

Playing well within one's own capability motivates golfers at all levels of proficiency to improve for personal satisfaction. Some have excelled far beyond others, leaving only perfection as the final goal—but they are few among many who have yet to develop their own potential. The difference between proficient golfers and others is not always inherent ability, but often only the ability of proficient golfers to establish accurate positions and help themselves by understanding their own golf swing. Many competent golfers, even experienced touring professionals, have commented occasionally that they experience difficulty because they know too little about their own golf swings.

The proficient, confident golfer recognizes the importance of understanding the swing and using fundamentals as a self-help method for continually keeping the swing intact. As an essential part of golf, this theoretical approach remains an untapped resource still available to the average golfer.

Although based on fundamentals, golf instruction in general does not always teach exactly what fundamentals are or why they are important in order that golfers may understand the importance of using fundamentals to establish accurate positions. Consequently, positions

The difference between proficient golfers and others is not always inherent ability, but often only the ability of proficient golfers to help themselves by understanding their own golf swing.

are often established incorrectly that preclude the ability of the swing to work with smooth coordination. Unless golfers understand the swing it is difficult to locate the source of trouble in order to isolate and correct the problem.

Building the basic golf swing presents fundamentals in sequence. This provides an opportunity to learn what fundamentals are, their purpose, how to apply them, where they are located in the swing, and how they affect each other. More important, however, while learning the use of fundamentals, golfers will be learning to help themselves—and helping golfers help themselves is the purpose of this book.

Although *Building Your Swing for Better Golf* was written expressly for the already established golfer rather than as an instructional book for beginners on how to play golf, student golfers are encouraged to build the swing as an accurate, precise method for developing a sound golf swing.

2

How Fundamentals Build a
Sound Golf Swing

Difficulty, frustration, and problems in golf are seldom caused by a lack of physical ability but rather by not understanding the swing so that one can establish and swing through positions that promote coordination. Anyone can play golf and, with practice, can play consistently well. Many golfers, however, fall victim to self-imposed problems by not having developed—or having had the advantage of developing—a golf swing based on fundamentals. Even limited ability can be used to the fullest extent, however, by learning to use fundamentals in sequence as presented through the book.

Understanding the cause of problems in golf promotes understanding of the importance of fundamentals, in that problems are generally caused by a combination of things that cause a poor golf swing and using fundamentals helps prevent problems. Golf, however, is surprisingly unique in a strange sort of way. Problems are frequently regarded as *results* of the swing rather than recognizing positions themselves as problems that result in incorrect movements. In other words, slicing may be mistakenly considered "the problem" rather than a combined incorrect grip and stance at address which caused an open clubface at impact. The result of such thinking is that rather than working toward understanding the overall swing in order to prevent or correct a combination of things, golfers are prone to subscribe to "quick tips" or "secrets" in golf to correct a *single* result of *several* poor positions. This is why many golfers, no matter how much they practice, continue to have problems.

The combination of inaccuracies that cause various problems in golf are neither prevented nor corrected by doing only a few things right. Problems are prevented by doing most things right and are corrected by correcting specific fundamentals that relate to specific problems. Applying fundamentals in sequence makes certain that all fundamentals are included, particularly when setting up to the ball, and prevents problems through the swing by establishing accuracy at address. Although problems are prevented by following guidelines at address, overcoming problems, which is also part of golf, is accomplished by having fundamental guidelines and checkpoints throughout the golf swing.

Building the swing by applying fundamentals in sequence is the same as building a house—and just as rewarding when finished. Just as a house can be prefabricated, wherein sections are joined together to complete the house, the golf swing can be built in sections and linked together to complete the swing. Both houses and golf swings, however, must be built on strong foundations and each section built independently strong within itself.

Units or sections of the swing (although always part of the whole) are the grip, position of address, backswing, downswing, and follow-through. Smaller sections are constructed to overlap and connect the larger units. The grip and position of address are the foundation for the swing and, because fundamentals build constantly on those that precede them, must be accurately established. Once the foundation is secured, fundamentals continue to build the following units, using the accuracy of preceding units to obtain overall accuracy through the swing. Units of the swing are connected with fundamental procedures such as the "waggle" and forward press, along with timing and rhythm. These, too, are developed in the building process.

Following the building process closely whether comparing, developing, or understanding the swing is important because small details are important. What may appear to be of little consequence may be of vast importance by either promoting or preventing coordination through the remainder of the swing. New fundamentals, when added, may change established positions, but these changes occur naturally and are part of the building process.

Although the shorter shaft of the seven iron is often preferred for practice, the five iron is used for instructional purposes throughout the book because the five iron establishes a *basic* position *from* which it is easier to learn to position and swing all of the other clubs. Learning fundamental procedures with the five iron develops a standard procedure that can easily be adapted to either longer or shorter clubs to position the ball, feet, and clubhead much more accurately.

Part 1
A Study of the Grip

3

Analyzing the Grip

An accurate grip is the most basically important ingredient in a reliable
golf swing, contributing about sixty percent to its overall efficiency.
Difficulty in other sections of the swing can frequently be traced
directly back to the grip because an incorrect positioning of the hands
may have restricted the *ability* of muscles in other parts of the body to
promote accurate coordination. That gives the false impression that the
difficulty lies somewhere other than in the grip itself. Because the grip is

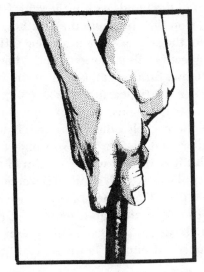

so basic, established golfers have generally developed one that is workable, though not necessarily one that is a contributing force in the swing as it should be. A study of the contribution the hands make as they relate to the basic swing, both separately and as a unit, can be beneficial even to those who know their grip to be correct.

The Vardon, or overlapping grip, positions the right little finger over the left forefinger and is rarely disputed as being the most popular put-together formula. The interlocking grip, however, which interlocks the left forefinger in between the last two fingers of the right hand, is equally effective. Although the book refers to the more common use of the overlapping grip, the principles applied relate to all golf grips, including the less common "ten-finger" grip, thus providing a better understanding of the use of them all.

Instructional books, and instructors too, generally teach the grip as a single, complete, and separate entity in the swing. They emphasize the position of the club in each hand separately and the importance of the accurate, unified relationship of the hands within the grip, but they do not always teach the full responsibility of the act of *assuming* the grip in establishing other positions. Although it may seem elementary and boringly repetitious (especially to experienced golfers), a study of the hands as separate fundamentals in separate chapters provides a new dimension of thought not usually obtained when simply "learning the grip." Although the grip is established for the obvious purpose of enabling the hands to work together, the grip itself and the act of completing the grip are closely related but different subjects because other positions are influenced when the hands are placed together.

In preparation for building the swing, Part One presents a study of the grip itself by analyzing the independent importance of each hand and the interrelated position of the hands within the grip. Because the right hand is positioned lower on the club than the left, however, extending the right arm to *complete* the grip exerts a muscular influence on other positions unless they are secured first. Consequently, Part Two separates the hands while introducing fundamentals that position the clubhead, feet, and lower body *before* the right arm moves to complete the grip.

Before a study of the grip begins, look at and study the hands. Although alike, they oppose each other, working independently yet together through muscular control. Throw a soft object such as a wad of paper in the air and hit it to the left with the palm of the right hand. The hand automatically pulls back with a little wrist action to either slap or hit the object for distance. The same objective, however, using the *left* hand, hits with the back of the hand; employing a natural firm-wristed "batting" effect. It strives to hit the object straight rather than far. Both hands hit "square" at impact, however, and the same natural use of the hands is employed in the swing, through the grip, by imparting this action to the clubhead. The left hand grip allows the left arm to keep the ball "on target" with backhanded firmness while the right hand grip allows the hand to "smack" the ball for distance.

Top performance in golf is not determined by brute force, but by coordination of muscles. Common sense dictates that as many as possible natural uses of muscles (which promote natural movement) be incorporated into the swing. The golf grip, as awkward as it seems, is not intended to be a naturally comfortable means for grasping the club, although it will become so with practice. It has been devised to promote accuracy and coordination throughout the golf swing. Golf clubs are only extensions of the arms and the grip is a sensibly constructed "tool" for transferring power from the body to the clubhead, through the hands. They must be accurately positioned, closely united, firm, and "active" to employ the natural use of the hands. An accurate grip develops confidence by promoting accuracy and coordination in a sound, *repeating* swing.

4

Fundamental #1—The Left Hand "Pistol" Grip

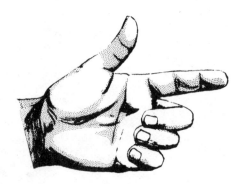

An accurate grip is the foundation for an accurate golf swing. Although any method of teaching will teach the same left hand grip as taught by the "pistol" grip, the pistol grip uses the natural conformity of the hand in a "shooting" position to establish the grip more naturally — and any method of teaching should obtain the same results.

How to Achieve Fundamental #1:

1. Center the clubhead on the ground
   with the shaft in line with the
   chin and steady the club with
   the right hand.

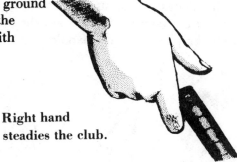

Right hand
steadies the club.

2. Assume a "shooting" position of the left hand. Point the forefinger
   straight ahead with the other three fingers in an open, "cupped"
   position and angle the thumb parallel to the three fingers.

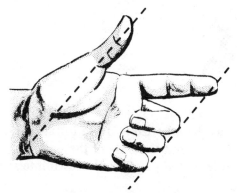

"Shooting" position
of left hand.

3. Extend the left arm to aim the forefinger alongside and straight
   down the shaft. Measure the top of the handle to the top joint of
   the thumb where the wrist breaks.

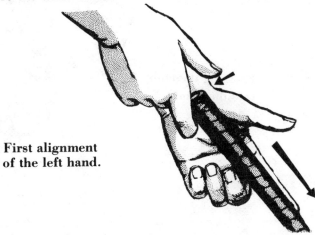

First alignment
of the left hand.

4. Keep the hand position the same and bend the wrist to cock the hand downward. The thumb, rather than the forefinger, will then aim alongside and straight down the shaft; the forefinger will point between the feet toward the heels; and the cupped fingers will be parallel to the handle.

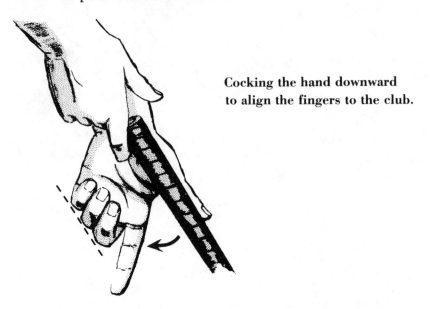

Cocking the hand downward
to align the fingers to the club.

5. Use the right hand to press the handle firmly down in the upper joints of the three cupped fingers and the base of the palm by pressing a small fold of skin from the palm firmly down into the last two fingers.

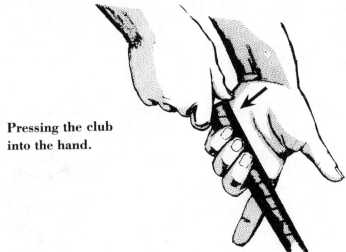

Pressing the club
into the hand.

6. Leaving the thumb and forefinger off the club, close the hand by gripping *up* with the fingers while pressing *down* with the heel pad of the hand. A tiny bit of the muscular pad should extend over the edge of the handle. The gripping action of the hand will cock the left wrist inward.

Firming the palm, three-finger grip.

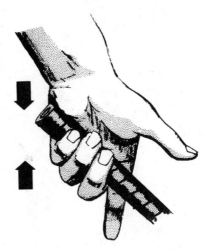

7. Drop the thumb straight down on top of the handle and *lightly* curl the forefinger around the handle of the club.

Closing the thumb and forefinger.

8. Press down slightly on the outside edge of the flat pad of the end of the thumb. Although the thumb remains on top, firming the grip will pinch the base of the "V" formed by the thumb and forefinger together and the line of the "V" will aim toward the right shoulder.

An accurate left hand grip points the "V" of the thumb and forefinger toward the right shoulder.

Purposes:

A. Cocks the hand into position to grip the club naturally while maintaining an upright stance.
B. Locks the club into position with "palm, three-finger grip."
C. Strengthens the left hand grip.
D. **Accurately positions the left thumb.**
E. Removes the left hand "pincer" fingers as a control factor in the swing.

A: Cocks the hand into position to grip the club naturally while maintaining an upright stance: Cocking the left hand downward to establish the left hand grip is a hinge action of the wrist that angles the fingers parallel to the diagonal line of the shaft, making it easy to grip the club naturally while keeping the stance upright. Keeping the stance upright promotes accuracy through the swing by establishing positions at address that promote good hand action and natural footwork. Although the grip itself may be correct, golfers frequently establish positions at address that affect the swing adversely by leaning over with

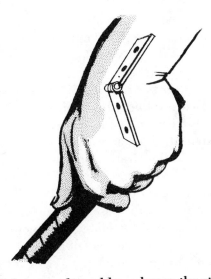

Hinging the left hand downward at address keeps the stance upright.

the hands cocked *upward* either to establish the grip or to position the clubhead.

Cocking the hands upward at address causes leaning over, frequently positioning the hands too low for good hand action; and leaning over too far moves the weight forward toward the toes, making it difficult

Addressing the ball with the left hand cocked downward (left) is an initial step in attaining accuracy at address and through the swing by preventing the body from leaning over to position the clubhead (right).

either to maintain balance or to shift the weight while swinging. The "pistol" grip, however, uses the natural angle of the left hand to establish accurate positions by cocking the left hand downward and keeping the stance upright.

B: Locks the club into position with "palm, three-finger grip:" The natural backhanded batting effect of the left hand uses natural muscular control to keep the ball "on target," and a strong left hand grip must be established at address to fortify the hand at impact. Strength combines with "feel" and maneuverability, however, by securing the club with the muscular pad of the heel of the hand and *gripping* the club with the fingers.

With the club secured at the base of the palm and the three fingers of the left hand firmly around the club, gripping *up* with the fingers and pressing *down* with the muscular pad of the heel of the hand will spread the muscle over and around the handle to lock it firmly into place. The left hand is immovably strong but the "feel" of the club is in the fingers.

A palm, three-finger grip presses the skin at the base of the palm either upward or downward, and accuracy can be determined by natural callouses which form at the extreme base of the palm next to the last two fingers of the left hand. By trying to avoid callouses at the base of the palm, a weaker grip is established by pushing the handle up under the heel pad. This places the club in the palm. Frequently, callouses form in the palm, which is indicative of an incorrect grip. Developing accurate callouses by *practicing* the grip is an uncomfortable but necessary part of a strong, accurate grip.

At the top of the swing, momentum through the backswing is "caught" and held by the hands, causing a short pause at the top of the swing for the transition of the backswing to the downswing. Unless the grip is particularly strong at the start of the swing, momentum forces the

An accurate left hand grip forms two callouses at the base of the palm.

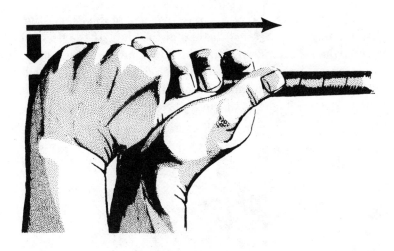

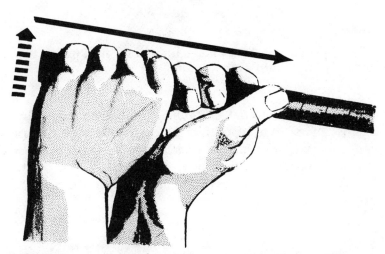

A firm palm, three-finger grip of the left hand at the top of the swing (top) prevents "dropping the clubhead" at the top (bottom).

left hand to let go and "drop the club" at the top as the downswing starts. Since it is virtually impossible to regain control of the clubhead *with* the left hand, the right hand tightens and grabs the loose club. When that happens, the left hand, in an effort to regain control, closes very sharply as the dropping action stops which bounces the clubhead upward from the top of the swing. The tightened right hand, in complete control of the club, throws the clubhead from the top either down on top of the ball or into the ground behind the ball.

C: Strengthens the left hand grip: A stronger grip is established for a full golf swing when a tiny bit of the muscular pad of the heel of the hand can be felt pressing back against the end of the club. If the tip of the handle is in the palm or extends beyond this bit of muscle, the left hand grip is not as strong. The strength of the three positions can be tested, with the three fingers firm, by pulling back and forth on the handle with the right hand. A stronger feeling can be detected when a little of the heel pad extends over the end of the club.

A stronger grip is obtained when a little of the heel pad of the left hand extends beyond the tip of the handle.

D: Accurately positions the left thumb: Golf jargon frequently refers to "long" or "short" thumb positions which describe their extension up or down the shaft. The left thumb is accurately positioned between the two simply by dropping it on the club.

Pressing down with the flat pad of the end of the thumb and pinching

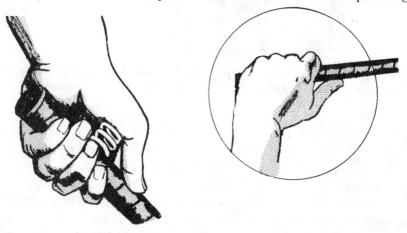

Springy flexibility of the left thumb at address (left) reinforces the grip at the top of the swing (right).

the base of the thumb and forefinger together further strengthens the left hand grip and creates a small triangular gap between the upper joint of the thumb and the club. This gives springy flexibility to the thumb while continuing to promote the "feel" and strength of the hand.

Positioning the thumb straight down the shaft at address positions it directly *under* the shaft at the top of the swing, reinforcing the hand, along with the firm three-finger grip, against "letting go" and "dropping the club" at the top of the swing. The shock absorber effect helps "hold" the position at the top during the transition of the backswing to the downswing.

An accurate wrist break through the backswing will keep the left wrist straight by cocking the left hand upward from the base of the thumb. Consequently, it is important to position the left thumb accurately for accuracy through the swing. Although golfers seldom grip the club with the left thumb too far left, the left hand is often positioned so far right—with the thumb on the right—that the left wrist bends inward through the wrist break.

E: Removes the left hand "pincer" fingers as a control factor in the swing: The pincer fingers are the thumb and end joint of the forefinger and their strength may be determined by any involvement of the two of them together. They must not be allowed to press tightly together or they become a control factor in the swing by *over*-controlling the clubhead.

Although the thumb and *hand* are pressed together in the left hand grip, pressing the thumb and *forefinger* together overcomes the inside muscles of the arm which are used in the swing by activating the outside muscles. The muscular difference can be felt in the arm by first tightening just the three fingers of the hand, then pressing only the thumb and forefinger together. Lightly curling the forefinger around the club prevents the pincer fingers from controlling the club but still enables the thumb to be as forceful as it should be.

5

Fundamental #2—The Right Hand Grip

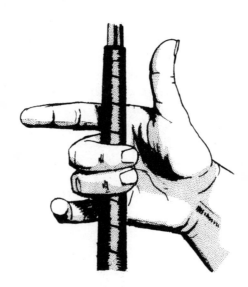

Although the left hand grip is established with the clubhead on the ground, it is easier to establish, strengthen, or check the right hand grip by extending the clubhead upward.

How to Achieve Fundamental #2:

1. Assume the left hand grip then hold the clubhead upward to position the right hand. With the palm of the right hand facing the left shoulder, place the shaded joint of the right hand (A) down firmly on the middle joint of the left forefinger (B). The little finger of the right hand will lie over the forefinger of the left (C).

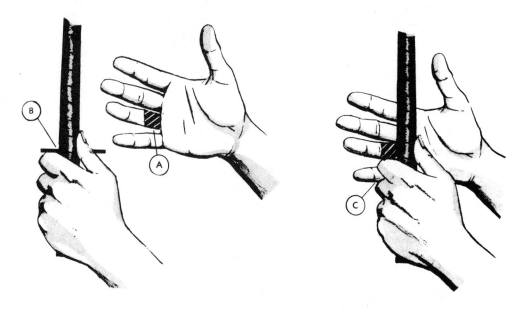

2. Keeping the right palm open, press the handle firmly into the fingers at the base of the palm with the left hand and wrap the two middle fingers tightly around the club. This draws the right hand up "square" to the handle so the little finger can be wiggled around to hook over the knuckle of the left forefinger.

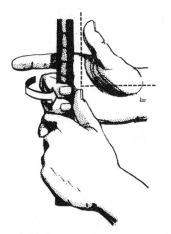

Gripping the club with the two middle fingers.

3. As the hand draws up and "squares" to the handle, the muscle pad of the palm at the base of the forefinger presses strongly against the handle. Draw the hand back slightly and press the handle even tighter into this firm position.

Securing the club at the base of the forefinger.

4. Press the base of the thumb and forefinger together and draw the palm of the right hand down and over the left thumb. The "spring" effect of the left thumb will be snugly in the cup of the palm of the right hand.

Drawing the right palm down and over the left thumb.

5. Firmly position the right thumb slightly offset to the left on the club and *lightly* close the forefinger.

Closing the thumb and forefinger.

6. The line of the "V" formed by the thumb and forefinger should aim toward the chin for an accurate right hand grip.

Purposes:

A. Uses natural angle of hand to establish right hand grip.
B. Strengthens the grip.
C. Develops "controlled" right hand power.
D. Accurately positions the right thumb.
E. Removes the right hand "pincer" fingers as a control factor in the swing.

A: Uses natural angle of hand to establish right hand grip: Holding the

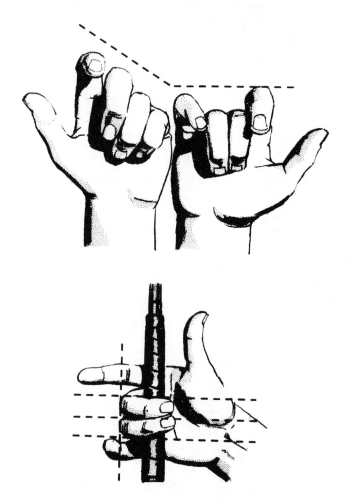

The angle of the hands is not the same when the grip is completed (top), making it easier to position the square right hand more accurately by holding the clubhead upward (bottom).

clubhead downward to establish the left hand grip places the handle at an angle which corresponds to the natural diagonal line of the hand. This makes it easy to grip the club naturally because the handle lies diagonally across the base of the palm. In the *completed* grip, however, the angle of the hands is not the same. As a result of gripping the club in the fingers, with the little finger *off* the shaft, the angle of the right hand is square rather than diagonal. It is easy to determine the angles by looking at the hands together as they would form their independent positions in the complete grip.

Experienced golfers almost instinctively raise the clubhead off the ground to grip the club more accurately.

Because it is difficult to position a square hand on a diagonal club, holding the clubhead *upward* to establish the right hand grip enables the right hand to be placed *squarely* against the handle—using the natural angle of the hand to comfortably grip the club more accurately. While setting up to the ball, experienced golfers almost instinctively raise the clubhead off the ground to grip the club more accurately.

Practicing the grip by frequently wiggling the hands together quickly develops a comfortable, familiar feeling which enables the grip to be completed with the club at any angle. It is also helpful in practice to grasp the club *above* the left hand grip, just as grasping a stick, then slide the right hand down into the grip described. This helps develop the feeling for an accurate right hand grip.

B: Strengthens the grip: The hands must be a closely knit unit through the swing to obtain accuracy and distance at impact. Regardless of how accurate the swing may be, somewhere along the way the hands will separate unless they are strongly united at address. The slightest separation will direct one hand (usually the dominant right hand) through the hitting zone with enough force to overpower the other at impact—losing distance or accuracy, or both, and frequently the ball as well!

Holding the clubhead upward and then placing the two middle fingers of the right hand down firmly on the left forefinger positions the hands close together. As the right hand completes the grip and the base of the thumb draws firmly against the hand, the two middle fingers roll sideways and downward, thus drawing the right hand down even closer to the left. Extending the clubhead upward to position the right hand develops a strong firm feeling for the grip, which is the same feeling that should be developed with the clubhead on the ground.

C: Develops "controlled" right hand power: The natural hitting capability of the right hand transfers into hitting power at impact, and "finger control" promotes strong right hand action as the hands release through the ball. The muscle pads of the hands play prominent roles in gripping the club with the fingers in both the left and right hand grip. Just as the heel pad of the left hand palm secures the club in the three fingers of the left hand, the right hand is reinforced by pressing the handle down under the palm muscle at the base of the forefinger. This secures the handle in the fingers of the right hand. Right hand power, however, which is dominant in right-handed golfers, must not be allowed to overshadow the less dominant left hand, which is the reason for positioning the little finger of the right hand off the club on top of the left forefinger.

Although the major role of the little finger of the right hand may appear to be that of strengthening the grip by locking the hands together, in reality the little finger has been "gotten rid of and given a job to do" in both the overlapping and interlocking grip. It serves a minor purpose in this regard, but it is actually removed from the shaft for the more important purpose of *weakening* the predominantly stronger right hand by intentionally removing some of its muscular capability. In golf instruction, a teaching professional will often strengthen the grip of a child or older person whose hands are not strong by placing all of the fingers and the thumbs on the club in a "ten-finger" grip. A regular "baseball" grip with the thumbs off the club should not

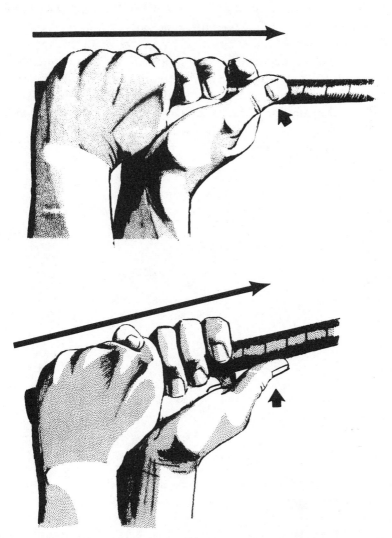

An offset right thumb at address positions the thumb offset at the top of the swing (top) which prevents bouncing the clubhead back too soon with the right thumb under the shaft (bottom). See page 42 (D)

be mistaken for the ten-finger grip because removing the thumbs from the club develops a weak golf grip.

D: Accurately positions the right thumb: The right thumb is slightly offset to the left at address for the reverse reason that the left thumb is positioned more on top of the shaft. The right hand reaches the top of the backswing before the left hand. With the *right* thumb under the shaft, just as the left, the swing action stops early and prevents completing the backswing. The same spring action found desirable in the left hand may cause the right hand to bounce the clubhead back too fast, "throwing the clubhead from the top" and ruining the timing of a smooth, controlled swing. (See illus. page 41.)

E: Removes the right hand "pincer" fingers as a control factor in the swing: Both hands must prevent the pincer fingers from controlling the clubhead by pressing the base of the thumbs and hands together but curling the forefingers lightly around the club. By lightly closing the forefingers, they become "feel" fingers—a short of sensory guide in the grip—but the tips of the forefingers will not join forces with the thumbs to overcontrol the club.

Part 2
The Position of Address

6

Analyzing the Position of Address

Addressing the ball correctly is the basic requirement for hitting a straight and accurate shot. Many golfers, however, encourage trouble before it starts because they have no guidelines to follow for the procedure at address adopted by more experienced golfers. Although years of experience, "feel," and confidence have replaced a need for experienced golfers to noticeably "build" the position, the position of address is not established all at once but rather by a series of exact fundamental positions established in thoughtful, overlapping sequences.

Incorporating fundamentals into the position of address in sequence automatically obtains objectives which are necessary before the swing is started: the clubface will be square to the line of flight; the posture upright; the grip and stance will be coordinated, squaring positions to the clubface and to the line of flight; the weight will be accurately distributed between and on the feet; the hands will be ahead of the ball; and the ball position will be measured accurately between and from the feet. It is not easy to attain these objectives unless positions are established in sequence to determine which objectives come first.

Golfers who have only a general knowledge of objectives and fundamentals may feel almost uncoordinated when establishing the position of address. It is not a matter of *being* uncoordinated, however, but *feeling* uncoordinated when trying to attain unknown objectives by applying some of the fundamentals randomly. The key to unlocking an uncoordinated feeling at address is the order in which all of the fundamentals are incorporated into the positions which attain specific objectives.

Golf terminology, as well as accurate positions, is an essential part of golf. Understanding the language helps understand the swing. Three terms used in golf frequently refer to positions of the shoulders, hips, feet, or face of the clubhead at address that are either "square," "open," or "closed" as they relate to each other and to the target line. Although the shoulders are a factor in accuracy at address and through the swing, they are not a factor in establishing the target line. Other than the right shoulder being lower than the left because the right *hand* is lower, the

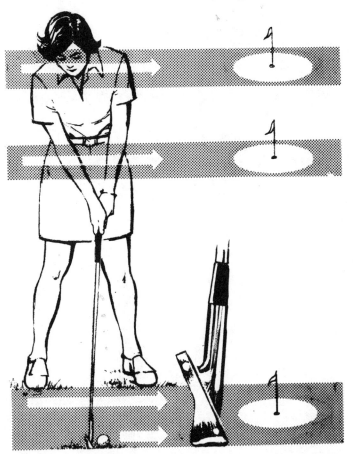

In order to hit the ball straight, the feet, hips, shoulders, and clubface must be square to one another and to the target line.

shoulders assume a square, open, or closed position similar to and as a result of other established positions.

The target line is established by two imaginary lines: a "line of flight" established by the clubface, which is the line on which the ball will travel, and a "directional line" established by the feet and hips that guides the clubhead through the swing.

In order to hit the ball straight, a square position of address must be established in the basic swing. This simply means that the clubface is aligned directly *down* a line of flight, directly toward the target, and positions of the feet, hips and shoulders are aligned directly *to* the line of flight.

The terms "open" and "closed" refer to positions aimed left or right of a line toward the target. When positions of the body *and* the clubface are aligned in the *same* direction, however, what "opens" positions of the

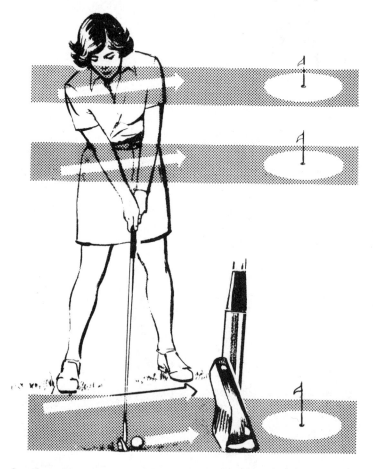

When the feet, hips, or shoulders aim left of the target line they are "open". When the clubface aims to the left, however, it is "closed".

body "closes" the face of the club. For instance, when the feet, hips, or shoulders aim *left* of the target line they are "open" to the target, but when the face of the *clubhead* aims to the left it is "closed."

The reverse is true with positions aimed to the right of the target line; the feet, hips, or shoulders are "closed" to the target but the face of the clubhead is "open."

Open and closed positions combine in many ways to hit both intentional and unintentional shots. If positions are established intentionally in order to "manipulate" the ball, the ball can be curved in flight—or hooked or sliced at will—by combining an open stance with an open clubface to slice to the right or a closed stance with a closed clubface to hook the ball to the left. More frequently, however, *in*correct positions are *un*intentionally established which hit the ball off-line, pulling straight left or pushing straight right as well as slicing or hooking.

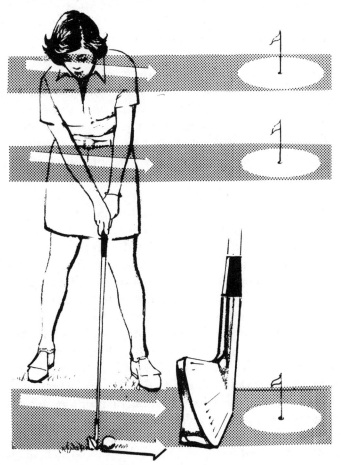

When the feet, hips, or shoulders aim right of the target line they are "closed". When the clubface aims to the right, however, it is "open".

The clubhead has a natural tendency to move into the backswing *on* the line established by the feet or hips—*especially* the hips—which greatly determines the angle at which the clubface strikes the ball. Because the clubhead generally returns the way it moves *into* the backswing, hitting the ball straight depends on starting a straight backswing—from a square position of address with parallel target lines.

A square position of address enables the clubhead to start straight back on the line of flight and return squarely through the ball, toward the target, because both the line of flight and directional line are parallel to each other and aim toward the target. Open or closed feet, hips, or shoulders, however, establish an angled directional line. Since the target lines are not parallel, the clubhead has no alternative but to start back on—and return *to*—an angle to *one* of the target lines. The ball will invariably be sliced or pushed to the right or hooked or pulled to the left. In a subconscious effort to *return* the clubface on the line of flight, which started out on an angled directional line, at the top of the swing the clubhead is frequently "looped" back *to* the line of flight to still mis-hit the ball as the swing pattern changes.

The average golfer should not be concerned with manipulating open and closed positions to intentionally finesse the ball, but should *avoid* establishing positions unintentionally which causes mis-hitting the ball. The need for hooking or slicing is almost nonexistent in the average golfer's game—at least while he is still an average golfer—and concentration should be applied to the shot most difficult of all to teach and learn, the one straight down the middle, by establishing square positions.

Soling the clubhead behind the ball is the "switch" which activates the mechanism of the swing. Since the clubface strikes the ball, it is the first alignment which must be "squared" to the target. The accuracy with which the clubhead is positioned determines the ability of fundamentals to continue establishing a precisely accurate position of address.

As positions are assumed, in sequence, the "waggle" (which is not a nervous "gimmick," but an important *part* of the swing) is used to "feel" positions into secure, interlocking relationship with each other by firmly adjusting independent positions and blending them all together to coordinate the swing. No amount of waggling, however, will benefit a golfer who is not establishing positions in sequence with specific purposes in mind. It is not difficult to waggle positions *out* of alignment if adjusting only to a comfortable position.

Learning and systematizing the procedure for addressing the ball correctly is not a "mind boggling" experience, regardless of the number of fundamentals involved. Once the procedure is developed—and practiced—the indecision of "which comes first" to obtain objectives will

Concentration is an important asset in golf and should not be wasted on something that can be relegated to the fundamentals.

be eliminated as a result of consistency in setting up to the ball the same way every time. When the position of address can be established quickly and confidently by *knowing* positions are correct, the mind is free to concentrate on other areas of the swing which cannot be structured by a formulated plan. Concentration is an important asset in golf and must not be wasted on something that can be relegated to the fundamentals.

The chapters devoted to addressing the ball present a comprehensive study of fundamental positions within the position of address, teaching the square position as the most dependable and teaching how to eliminate doing the *wrong* thing by automatically doing what is *right*. The process is an asset which no dedicated golfer can afford to be without.

7

Fundamental #3—The Basic Position at Address

Stepping up to the ball is so elementary that the action is not always regarded as being of fundamental importance. Stepping up to the ball promotes additional accuracy, however, by stepping *into* an accurate position (although it is difficult to step into an accurate position without first understanding objectives). Establishing a basic position while providing a foundation to build on helps set up to the ball more accurately by learning certain objectives.

Most golfers eventually develop some sort of personal "style" or system for stepping up to and addressing the ball, although without the same objectives in mind the "styles" may vary considerably. Experienced golfers, however, address the ball in a somewhat similar manner mainly because, having become experienced, they use fundamentals in a somewhat similar manner to obtain similar results. Establishing and understanding the basic position in golf is an important step in learning how to consistently be *able* to address the ball in a "professional manner" by *practicing* obtaining the same professional objectives.

How to Achieve Fundamental #3:

Assume a basic position of standing "at attention." Stand tall and straight with the feet together and the arms relaxed. Pull in the stomach and tuck the hips under to pull the weight toward the heels.

Purposes:

A. Establishes a "square" relationship of the feet to the hips.
B. Keeps the weight off the toes.
C. Promotes an upright stance.
D. Provides the foundation for a natural pivot.

A: Establishes a "square" relationship of the feet to the hips: Standing at "attention," align the feet and hips parallel to each other. Although nothing should occur to change this relationship, the one position which can *inadvertently* change is the square position of the hips which *must* remain square at address. Unlike the feet which retain the square position, the hips are easily influenced to change by the slightest movement of muscles when other positions are established, particularly toward being turned "open" toward the target.

Muscular movement is directed toward the left when setting up to the ball. (See Fundamental #7A in Chapter 11). With the body structured so the hips swivel comfortably between the stationary position of the feet and shoulders, it is not uncommon for the hips to slip into an open position because they, too, want to "go" in the direction of the target. Should this happen, however, the right hip will be in the way as the backswing starts, blocking both the hip and shoulder turn as the hips move laterally rather than turning rotationally. With the right hip in the way, it is difficult to start an accurate swing pattern by starting the clubhead on the line of flight and swinging onto the directional line.

The sequence in which fundamentals are presented is designed to establish square positions and protect the hips, especially, from slipping into an open position. The hips can then turn rotationally from the start of the swing rather than blocking a natural turning movement. As positions are established, knowing the hips *can* be influenced to change affords an opportunity to guard against it.

B: Keeps the weight off the toes: The strongest feeling in the feet occurs when they are positioned to spring forward from a position on the toes which encompasses a naturally strong flexing of the leg muscles. Inexperienced golfers—particularly those who are athletically adept at using the feet—are often enticed into establishing this stronger forward position, but it is not a good foundation for the swing.

Tucking the hips under at address pulls the weight toward the heels, not to establish the weight on the heels but to keep it off the toes while setting up to the ball. As additional fundamentals continue to build the position, the hips relax somewhat, the seat sticks out a bit, and the weight moves slightly forward. Meanwhile, however, it is good exercise for those who establish the weight on the toes to *feel* how it feels on the heels. Although the weight is not entirely on the heels at address, it must definitely *not* be on the toes.

Swinging a club in a full swing arc generates tremendous momentum and, if given the opportunity, momentum will force the body off balance. Accurate weight distribution from heels to toes, however, maintains balance while swinging by coordinating the action of the feet with the action of the swing. Keeping the weight off the toes places the center of gravity toward the heels, promoting good footwork, strong relaxed legs, and a natural pivot—all of which are needed to transfer weight and maintain balance through the golf swing.

In order to sense the feeling for a balanced golf swing—and for balance comparison between the heels and toes—separate the feet, extend the arms horizontally, and swing the arms around to turn the body left and right. Exaggerate the movement: first, with the weight far forward on the toes, then with the weight back toward the heels. It is easy to determine that better balance is maintained with the weight toward the heels, activating the "feeling" in the balls of the feet. Keeping the weight toward the heels, flex the knees while swinging the arms around and let the hips turn and the legs "flow" along with the movement. The balls of the feet "feel and catch" the weight shift and turning movement, easily maintaining balance and transferring the weight back and forth as the heels lift off the ground. It is that exact feeling which should be developed, using natural muscular control for a strong and balanced swing.

C: Promotes an upright stance: Standing upright at address produces a natural pivot and a balanced, upright swing, and standing at "attention" is a basic position from which the upright stance evolves. Assuming an upright stance, however, is sometimes difficult—particularly if only observing other golfers—because the *appearance* of a golfer at address is that of leaning over from the waist to position the clubhead. Bending from the waist to position the club, however, before the knees are bent, will keep the legs straight, move the weight forward, and establish poor positions.

Although the upper body does bend slightly when setting up to the ball, fundamentals establish and maintain an upright stance by lowering the body from the knees, keeping the weight back toward the heels *before* leaning over to complete the grip and stance. Meanwhile, standing upright at address helps establish accurate positions.

D: Provides the foundation for a natural pivot: A natural pivot is the result of square positions at address which enable the hips to turn, rather than move laterally, as the backswing starts. Although a natural movement that starts a balanced, upright swing, pivoting is difficult if positions are open at address and the hips are unable to turn along with other beginning movements. The basic position of standing at "attention" provides a foundation for a natural pivot.

8

Fundamental #4—Positioning the Clubhead

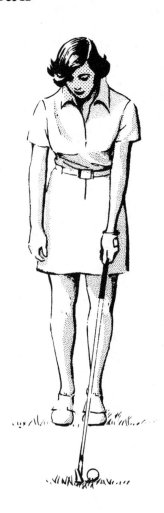

Soling the clubhead behind the ball is the beginning movement of the swing itself. The accuracy with which it is done determines the ability of future fundamentals to continue building a sound golf swing.

The straight arm-shaft position required to position the clubhead behind the ball will be changed by the addition of later fundamentals, but this position—at this point in the swing—is an important step in building an accurate position of address:

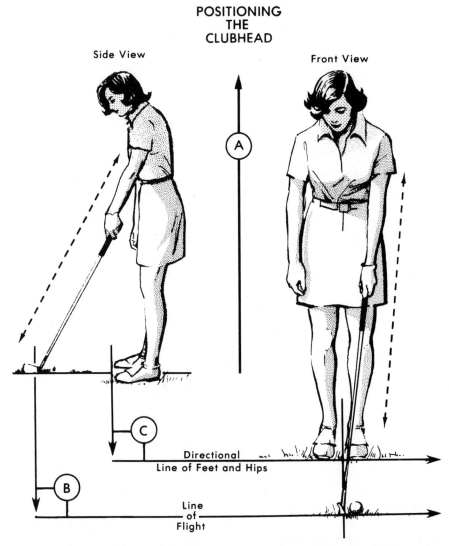

POSITIONING
THE
CLUBHEAD

Side View

Front View

A

C

Directional
Line of Feet and Hips

B

Line
of
Flight

Learning a basic procedure for positioning the clubhead will keep the stance upright (A) and establish an accurate target line by squaring the clubface to the target (B) and squaring positions to the clubface (C).

How to Achieve Fundamental #4:

1. Form a cross on the ground, using three-foot tape or string, and aim the horizontal line toward a definite target. Nails can be tied to strings to secure them on the ground.

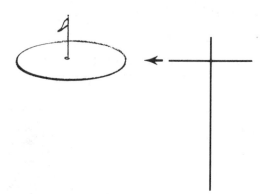

2. Straddle the vertical string with the heels together and the toes parallel to the horizontal string.

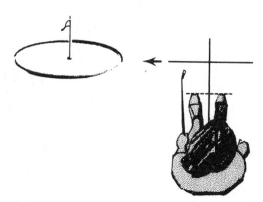

3. Without leaning over and using only the left hand grip, comfortably extend the left arm and shoulder so the arm and shaft are in a straight line with each other. Keep the stance upright and adjust the feet along the vertical string until the clubhead can be centered where the two strings cross. Align the bottom edge of the clubface *on* the vertical string, "squaring" the center of the clubface toward the target to establish the "line of flight."

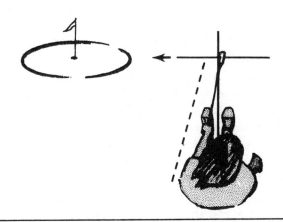

4. Secure the third string along the toes parallel to the feet and to the line of flight to establish a "directional line."

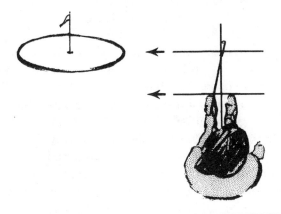

Purposes:

A. Determines the target line.
B. Squares the clubface to the line of flight.
C. Measures radius of the swing.
D. Measures how far to stand from ball.
E. Positions hands ahead of ball.
F. Places sole of club squarely on the ground.
G. Protects positions already established.
H. Establishes a relaxed but strong position.
I. Helps square the shoulders at address.

A: Determines the target line: Two lines establish the target line; a line of flight established by the clubface, and a directional line established by the feet. The line of flight aims toward the target and the lines are parallel to each other. In order to hit the ball straight, the clubface must first be squared to the target in order to establish the line of flight (or the line the *ball* will follow) and the feet then squared to the line of flight to establish the directional line (or the line the *clubhead* will follow). Although both lines form the target line, each line is independently important in obtaining accuracy, both at address and through the swing. Using strings to establish the lines is an accurate method used for learning how to "square up the ball" as well as for learning how to swing the clubhead on the target line.

B: Squares the clubface to the line of flight: The primary requirement for hitting an accurate golf shot is first determining the line of flight from the ball toward the target and then squaring the bottom edge of the clubface at a direct right angle to that imaginary line. It is not always easy in golf, however, to "sight" an accurate target line while standing sideways at address, although using strings and *practicing* helps develop both subconscious and visual accuracy for lining up correctly. Learning to sight from behind the ball, first with the use of strings, develops a feeling for "seeing" the line more clearly when strings are no longer used. Those who still have difficulty lining up accurately may find it helpful to spot some point on the line just in front of the ball and then square the clubface to that point which is still on line with the target.

C: Measures radius of the swing: The word "radius" is defined as "a straight line going from the center to the outside of a circle," such as a spoke in a wheel. Since the length of the radius determines the size of the circle, the golf swing radius determines the swing arc—and the radius is *measured* at address by extending the left arm in line with the shaft while the feet are together and the stance upright. The golf swing radius should never be larger or smaller than a comfortable, full extension of the left arm at address for two important reasons: (1) to build clubhead speed with a maximum swing arc; and (2) to return the clubhead to the exact location of the ball.

If the left arm is bent or extended too far at address, there is physical leeway *through* the swing for the arms to adjust to a longer or shorter extension. Such a leeway changes the arc of the swing by lengthening or shortening its radius, and thus prevents the clubhead from returning accurately.

The swing radius, once measured, will remain the same because the arms maintain the radius by remaining extended through the swing—the left arm through the backswing and the right arm in the follow through. In order to return the clubhead accurately, however, the swing radius must be measured accurately at address.

D: Measures how far to stand from ball: Comfortably extending the left arm to position the clubhead—with the feet together and the stance upright—measures exactly how far to stand from the ball when using any or every club. The length of the shaft of different clubs will extend the distance for the woods and shorten the distance for the irons, from the driver through the wedge.

Overextending the arms by reaching too far for the ball has a tendency to pull the weight forward. This prevents maintaining balance while swinging. Crowding the arms by not extending the left arm, "hunches" the shoulders, positions the ball too close and restricts a full extension of the arms while swinging. Either position will return the clubhead incorrectly to hit on the heel or toe of the club because the swing adjusts the clubhead to the more neutral position at impact.

E: Positions hands ahead of ball: Positioning the clubhead with just the left hand and the arm and shaft in a straight line places the left hand ahead of the ball in the position of address. When the right hand completes the grip, both hands will still be forward and, with correct swing movements, will return to the same position. Accuracy is obtained with the hands ahead of the ball at address and ahead of the ball at impact. Positioning the clubhead with the *left* hand prevents inadvertently positioning the hands behind the ball as a result of positioning the clubhead with the *right* hand.

Since muscles have a strong natural tendency to return to original positions, positioning the hands forward is the best assurance that they will be leading through the hitting zone. Although additional procedures used in setting up to the ball also make certain the hands are well forward before the backswing starts, *positioning* the hands forward promotes more accuracy by preventing unnecessary adjustments which may change the original alignment.

Although an apparently trivial matter, the position of the hands determines whether the clubhead is pushed into the backswing or pulled away from the ball. Pushing the clubhead away from the ball with a firm left arm, as opposed to pulling the club back with the hands, is an important fundamental procedure. It turns the shoulders and the hips and keeps the clubface "square." Pushing is very difficult with the hands behind the ball because the hands are positioned to *pull.*

Pulling the clubhead away from the ball—wherein the hands start first before the clubhead leaves the ball—prevents a natural hip and shoulder turn by pulling the body laterally. The pulling movement pulls the weight across the right foot, which causes topping the ball at impact (as it is difficult to get *off* the right foot on the downswing). If the weight should transfer back to the left, which is essential to the golf swing, a whipping action of the clubhead through the backswing and downswing will occur. This will "loop" the clubhead at the top of the swing,

Positioning the clubhead with the *right* hand may inadvertently position the hands behind the ball at address (left) rather than accurately ahead of the ball by positioning the clubhead with the *left* hand (right).

changing the clubface angle and returning the clubface open to slice, push, shank, or "toe" the ball off to the right at impact. Quick hand action at impact, however, may quickly close the clubface to hook or pull the ball instead.

The hands must be ahead of the ball for another reason, but it is better defined by understanding the construction of the golf club itself. Golf clubs are constructed for the *purpose* of having the hands forward at address and ahead of the ball at impact, a distinctive feature not easily determined by golfers and not always considered when setting up to the ball. Unless golfers are aware of this, a great deal of difficulty may be encountered in trying to address the ball correctly with the clubface square. If golfers have found a way to square the clubface to the target with the hands *behind* the ball, they may also find they have removed the built-in power of the club by "laying the club back flat." Addressing the ball with the hands behind the ball changes the loft of a five iron, for instance, to that of a six. Combined with other inaccuracies, the additional loft of the clubface will either "scoop" the ball skyward or top the ball by "scooping" up on the ball at impact. Angling the shaft of the club forward by positioning the *hands* forward makes it far easier to establish accurate positions as well as hit the ball more accurately.

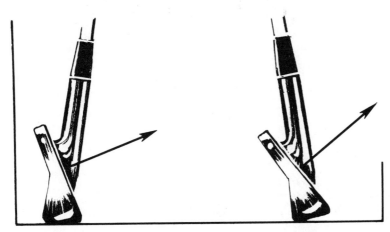

The hands must be ahead of the clubhead at address, angling the shaft of the club forward (left) to prevent changing the loft of the club-face—changing the loft of the five iron, for instance, to that of the six (right).

F: Places sole of club squarely on the ground: Hitting accurately and squarely in the center of the clubface also depends upon soling the clubhead squarely on the ground at address. Occasionally the clubhead is positioned with the toe or heel up off the ground, but the clubhead returns in the same position, hitting the ball *on* the heel or toe and misdirecting the shot when the club turns slightly in the hands at impact.

A toe-up or heel-up position at address generally indicates incorrect positions which bow the wrists too high or position the hands too low. Leaning over from the waist and bending over too far positions the club on the heel. Standing too upright or playing the ball in too close keeps the wrists too high and positions the club on the toe. Standing upright with the feet together and soling the clubhead behind the ball with a straight left arm, however, soles the clubhead squarely on the ground.

There is another factor which determines the ability of the golfer to be *able* to sole the clubhead squarely on the ground and still establish an

Following a basic procedure for setting up to the ball prevents establishing poor positions that position the ball or clubhead incorrectly.

accurate position of address—the "lie" of the club itself. Golf clubs must "fit" the golfer, and the majority of golfers will have no difficulty using a standard length club. Unusually tall or short golfers, however, should be particularly careful not to establish poor positions at address by adapting their swings to clubs which naturally assume a toe-up or heel-up position.

The height of the golfer, swing ability, and personal preference should determine the length of the shaft, which may vary by one or two inches. If the clubhead cannot easily be soled squarely on the ground, however, by comfortably extending the left arm in a straight line with the shaft while the feet are together and the stance upright, it may indicate that either the shaft of the club is too long or short for the height of the golfer. It may also indicate that the lie of the club itself is incorrect for the height of the golfer.

Golf professionals are fully qualified to "fit" equipment to the golfer and should be consulted if the clubhead cannot comfortably be soled squarely on the ground by the procedure used in building the position of address. The length and lie of the club as well as shaft flexibility, swing weight, and overall weight of the club can be determined for each individual golfer. It is worth remembering that proper equipment is certainly an asset in golf.

G: Protects positions already established: Unless a golfer is extremely familiar with what he is trying to accomplish, it is difficult to keep the stance upright, make the proper alignment of the clubhead and the body, and position the ball correctly in relationship to the hands and feet—particularly if the ball is addressed with a completed grip and the feet already separated. The tendency is to lean over at address with the weight on the toes and establish poor positions which then need correction.

If difficulty is encountered in establishing accurate positions while setting up to the ball, the left-handed, feet-together technique described is an excellent procedure to follow when actually playing golf.

H: Establishes a relaxed but strong position: Maintaining a firm left hand grip, comfortably extending the left arm to position the clubhead, retaining an erect stance with the weight toward the heels all develop a relaxed but strong position of address.

A *comfortable* extension of the left arm at address determines the ability of muscles of the entire upper body to flex correctly throughout the swing. Muscles must continue contracting on the backswing to develop body torque and they cannot work efficiently if they are strained beyond a comfortable firmness at address. The arms must also have *some* tension, however, for strength to initiate the swing. This is automatically provided by the straight arm-shaft position. Good timing results from just the right amount of "relaxed firmness," and a sound golf swing begins with addressing the ball in a relaxed but strong position.

I: Helps square the shoulders at address: All of the foregoing benefits are derived simply by extending the left arm in a straight line with the shaft. However, keeping the hips square and letting the left shoulder move *forward* when positioning the clubhead will square the shoulders at address when the right arm is positioned. Keeping the left shoulder *back* as the left arm extends establishes an *open* shoulder position by enabling the right arm to pull the right shoulder ahead of the left when the grip is completed. Just as open hips position the right *hip* in the way, an open shoulder position will place the right *shoulder* in the way as the backswing starts. Either open position starts a lateral rather than turning movement as the clubhead leaves the ball by blocking the shoulder turn and pivot.

Squaring the shoulders at address helps return the shoulders square for accuracy through the ball. An open position, however, encourages the right shoulder to move forward from the *top* of the swing in an effort to return to the same position as established at address. "Coming over the top" and swaying through the backswing may either be prevented or corrected by keeping the hips square with the weight toward the heels and letting the left shoulder move forward as the left arm extends when positioning the clubhead.

9

Fundamental #5—Separating the Feet

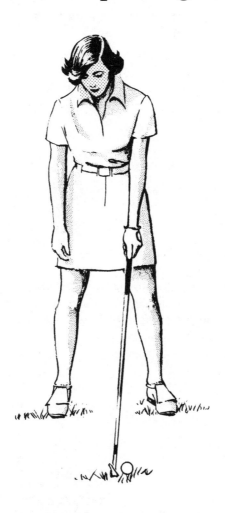

The importance of the seemingly insignificant act of separating the feet at address is frequently lost in a broader discussion on stance or posture, either of which may explain the position of the feet but seldom the reasons or benefits derived from positioning the feet with deliberate accuracy. Although several important purposes are attained, of primary importance is that separating the feet from the *clubhead*—by positioning the clubhead first—positions the *ball* more accurately. The five iron should continue to be used for instructional purposes, but the fundamental procedure for separating the feet applies to the use of all golf clubs.

How to Achieve Fundamental #5:

1. Reestablish positions on the parallel lines as described in the preceding chapter.

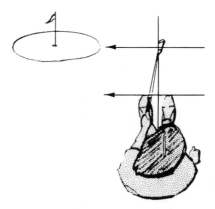

2. Separate the feet by moving *first* the left foot, *then* the right, to the width of the shoulders. Position the toes on the horizontal string, pointing straight ahead, and *center the clubhead positioned directly between the heels.*

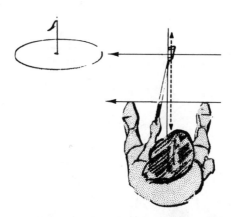

3. *Keep the heels in place* and angle the feet outward by moving the left toes four inches and the right toes one. In effect, the right foot is "closed" in relationship to the left foot (which moves a little bit "open" and a little "off-line"). Since the center of the stance will be measured from the heels (which remain on-line), when the toes angle outward the width of the five iron will still be centered directly between the heels.

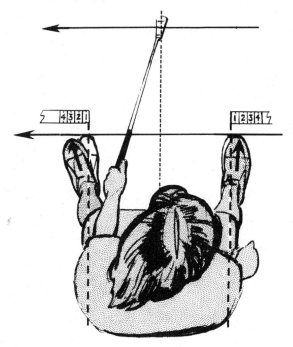

Positioning the feet at address.

Purposes:

A. Distributes weight equally between the feet.
B. Protects positions already established.
C. Squares feet to line of flight.
D. Determines angle of feet.
E. Determines width of stance.
F. Positions ball correctly.

A: Distributes weight equally between the feet: Good footwork is needed in golf in order to shift the weight to the right on the backswing, then back to the left on the downswing to pull the arms down from the top and back through the hitting zone, and weight transference is easier when the weight is equal at address. Because of the keen sensory feeling in the feet, however, it is not difficult to set up incorrectly while feeling that the weight is equal—*unless* the left foot is positioned before positioning the right. The weight can be almost entirely on one foot, but the "feel" of the other will make the weight seem equal.

Positioning the left foot first at address may appear to be of little importance, but the foot that is positioned first will transfer weight in that direction and establish the weight firmly on that foot. The right side, being predominantly stronger than the left, will retain the greater percentage of weight on the right foot if the right foot is positioned first

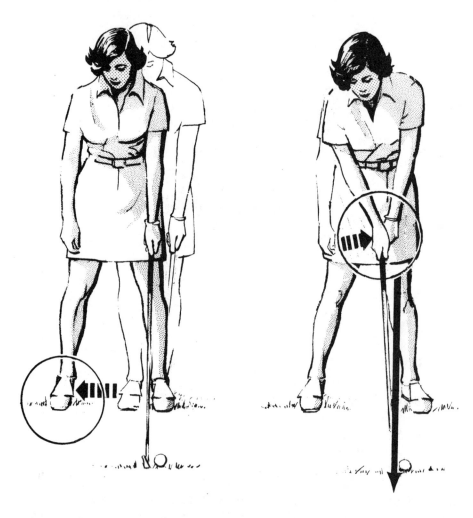

Incorrectly positioning the right foot first at address (left) establishes a comfortable position from which the *left* foot may not move at all, establishing poor positions by positioning the hands behind the ball and pushing the hips open as the right hand completes the grip (right).

even when the left foot moves forward, and it is difficult to get off the right foot on the downswing. Positioning the *left* foot first, however, changes the situation. Although the weight shifts to the left, the dominant right side will pull its share of weight back to the right and automatically distribute the weight equally between the feet.

The weight must shift to the right on the backswing in order to shift back to the left on the downswing, but weight transference is sometimes confusing to golfers who know that swaying, which moves the body laterally, is a disruptive force in the swing. Swaying is prevented, however, by the shoulder turn and pivot as the weight shifts back and forth, and swaying is too frequently corrected or prevented incorrectly by golfers who set the weight on the left or right and try to keep it there.

Establishing the weight on the left foot at address may keep the weight on the left while swinging and change the arc of the swing as the body lowers and raises, or the weight may "kick" off the left foot onto the right as the downswing starts in a "reverse weight shift." Establishing the weight on the right foot keeps the weight on the right on the downswing which causes the same adverse results as a reverse weight shift—"falling away from the ball" and "throwing the club from the top."

B: Protects positions already established: A quick change in the position of the left hand and the hips may occur if the right foot is positioned first: as the right foot moves to the right, it also shifts the weight to the right and pulls the left hand back behind the ball. With the weight then established on the strong right side rather than the body shifting from what *feels* like a comfortable position, the left foot may not move at all. Consequently, the feet just stay where they are—with the weight on the right—when the right arm extends to complete the grip. Since the clubhead is off the heel of the left foot, however, rather than between the feet, either the right hand extends too far to complete the grip (pushing the hips "open") or the left hand may move closer to the right hand to establish the grip more comfortably. This positions the left hand farther behind the ball and eventually positions both hands incorrectly. Adjusting positions into accuracy from such inaccuracy makes it difficult to keep the clubface square while setting up to the ball.

Positioning the left foot first at address is ample protection for distributing the weight equally between the feet, keeping the hips and clubface square with the hands ahead of the ball, and positioning the ball and clubhead accurately between the feet.

C: Squares feet to line of flight: Separating the feet with the toes on the horizontal string accurately squares the feet to a square clubface and to the line of flight, thus establishing the directional line and completing the target line. Although both the line of flight (established by the clubface) and the directional line of the feet are horizontally the same at address, which is determined before the toes angle outward; establishing a line of flight with the clubface *before* establishing the directional line with the feet is a far more accurate procedure for addressing the ball correctly. Positioning the feet first will generally require repositioning the feet, which makes it much more difficult to obtain an accurate alignment.

Both horizontal lines are necessary to start a good swing pattern because the clubhead starts back on the line of flight but quickly swings upward and back *onto* the directional line. It is difficult to initiate a good swing pattern unless the line of flight and directional line of the feet and hips are parallel at address.

Using strings to square the clubface is an excellent learning method. When visual sight replaces the strings, however, it is not uncommon for even experienced golfers to fall into a habit of lining up incorrectly with either the clubface or the feet. If hitting consistently left or right, the string technique can be used to check for accuracy, even when playing golf, by using a club instead of strings to check the accuracy of alignment:

Checking the accuracy of alignment at address.

Using the principle of diminishing lines—in which two parallel lines such as railroad tracks appear to meet in the distance—square the clubface to a far-away target for the diminishing line effect, then square the feet to the square clubface with the angle of the feet the same. Complete the position of address, then lay the club down on the ground along the line of the toes and sight from behind the club. If the shaft aims toward the target, both the feet and the clubface are accurately aligned. If not, repeat the procedure and make corrections until the alignment is accurate, then practice the new setup.

D: Determines angle of feet: Part of the difficulty encountered by golfers in establishing a square position of address stems from the fact that the word "square" is somewhat ambiguous in relationship to the feet. Although the feet themselves are squared to the line of flight, the *angles* of the feet are not. Understanding the difference helps position the feet correctly.

As well as stance positions (pages 46 and 47), there are angles of the feet. The feet angle "open" when the toes point outward (A) and they are "square" or "closed" when they point straight ahead (B). A stance *position*, however, is not determined by the angle of the feet but rather by the alignment of the heels to the target line. An "open stance," for instance, (from a square stance position), moves the left foot off the target line by moving the heel position (C); whereas, "angling the left foot open" moves the *toes* off-line but keeps the *heel* in place to maintain the stance position (D). Establishing and checking square alignments before the angle is set is one of the keys to a square position.

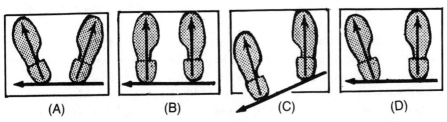

(A)   (B)   (C)   (D)

The angle of the feet has a critical influence on the swing by either restricting or releasing both the backswing and the follow-through. The right foot is slightly closed to restrict the backswing movement and the left foot is slightly open to release the follow-through.

Before discussing the angle of the feet, a thought to remember in golf is that nothing in the golf swing should be carried to an extreme. There is always an exact "just right" position or movement which promotes coordination. Although the feet are open and closed in relationship to each other, neither should be entirely open nor entirely closed. *Over-*

establishing positions as well as overcorrecting the swing are common mistakes in golf. Little adjustments make big differences in the swing and "slightly" is an expression used to encourage subtlety in both the physical and mental approach to establishing, adjusting, or correcting not only the angle of the feet but any position or movement.

The right foot: A slightly closed right foot at address provides a variety of assets in the swing by restricting the backswing movement.

(1) *A slightly closed right foot promotes a natural pivot and prevents the lateral "sway":* Power in the golf swing comes from winding up the body and creating tension of the muscles between the shoulders and the hips. This tension unwinds with tremendous force, generating clubhead speed as the weight shifts back to the left and the arms are pulled down from the top. An *open* right foot at address prevents this buildup of power by allowing the hips to move laterally into the backswing as the shoulders turn. *Closing* the right foot, however, blocks the lateral movement and prevents the body from sliding, or "swaying," by forcing the hips to turn.

As the clubhead starts into the backswing, the shoulder turn becomes automatic as a result of pushing the clubhead through the backswing. The *shoulders* then turn the *hips.* A natural shoulder turn and pivot combine to build up power, but *only* if the right foot prevents the lateral movement by being closed at address.

(2) *A slightly closed right foot promotes an upright swing:* An upright swing establishes accurate positions at the top of the swing to help return the clubhead squarely through the ball. Swinging upright instead of "flat" results from a series of correct positions which also promote a natural shoulder turn and pivot, one of which is the closed right foot which prevents the lateral sway.

(3) *A slightly closed right foot helps keep the head steady:* Fundamentals position the head behind the ball at address, and keeping the head steady in the same relative position is an important pivotal position which enables the coiling mechanism of the body and the hitting action of the hands to coordinate at impact. A bobbing or moving head, however, is not the *cause* of problems. A moving head is simply an indication that the entire body is moving back and forth or up and down which pulls the head off-line.

A closed right foot, which prevents swaying laterally, helps keep the head steady and prevents releasing power somewhere other than through the hitting zone. When the head moves laterally through the backswing, the weight moves laterally across the right foot and generally stays on the right on the downswing. When that happens, the hands release too soon, pulling the shoulders, arms, and hands *up* through the hitting zone, which causes "looking up" by pulling the head up, too. The other alternative, swaying back through the ball, pulls the head forward beyond the impact area, and the hands release a shade too late to release the hitting power.

A moving head and "looking up" are both indications of a lateral sway. Closing the right foot, however, turns the body rotationally, whereupon the head remains down and steady as the pivotal point in the swing.

(4) *A slightly closed right foot allows a transfer of weight to the right on the backswing and provides a solid position to push against to shift the weight back to the left on the downswing:* Bracing the right foot against the movement of the backswing will "catch and hold" the backswing movement as the weight shifts to the right, storing power and releasing it with additional force as the body springs away from the braced right foot and shifts the weight to the left.

(5) *A slightly closed right foot promotes good timing by preventing overswinging:* Good timing at the top of the swing promotes a movement of the lower body back to the left as the initial downswing movement. Restricting the backswing movement with a slightly closed right foot promotes good timing by promoting good footwork and lower body action. Angling the right foot too far open, however, results in an unrestricted backswing which prevents good timing either by swaying or overswinging.

Overswinging with the hands, arms, and clubhead, as a result of angling the right foot open, makes it difficult for lower body action to sense the "feeling" necessary for starting the downswing action. Blocking the backswing action, however, with a slightly closed right foot, results in good timing by restricting lower body action which prevents the upper body from swinging too far.

(6) *A slightly closed right foot promotes good rhythm with relaxed and supple legs:* A rhythmical swing is promoted by a rhythmical swinging movement of relaxed and supple legs. The legs, however, must be free of tension at address and through the swing which is partly predetermined by the right foot position.

With the exception of the tension factor at address, the angle of the right foot could be entirely closed. With the left foot angled open, however, and the hips square at address, a small amount of tension develops in the inside muscles of the right leg with the foot entirely closed. As slight as the feeling is, one of two things occur: either the hips relieve the tension by slipping into an open position, or the right leg stays twisted at address and defies relaxation. Angling the right foot just a little bit open, however, relieves the strain on the inner leg muscles to keep the hips square and the legs relaxed, but still provides a braced foot position for the backswing action.

The left foot: The angle of the left foot at address frequently determines the golfer's ability to complete the swing and receive the transfer of weight from the right side to the left. Although the left foot is angled open in relationship to the right, the position must not be *over*-established into an exaggerated open position.

Following through: Completing the swing is not always what golfers *do* but what they are *able* to do by establishing correct positions. Muscles wind up through the backswing and unwind on the downswing. It is the winding and unwinding process that transmits body torque into clubhead speed as the weight shifts left and the hips turn through the ball. Following impact, however, the swing dissolves into a free, fluid movement. This movement must not be restricted by a closed left foot in order to keep the clubhead accelerating through the ball with a full follow-through.

Closing the left foot at address blocks out the ability of the left hip to turn on the downswing and follow through. Rather than "releasing" the swing and letting the hips turn through the ball, a closed left foot causes the body to move laterally on through the ball. Unless the left foot is angled open when addressing the ball, the swing cannot be completed and the clubhead will not be accelerating squarely through the ball at impact.

Although the left foot angles outward, *exaggerating* the position encourages the hips to spin back through the hitting zone too far, too soon, pulling the clubhead inward from the target line. Rather than hitting straight on through the ball, the clubhead either pulls or slices the ball according to the angle of the clubface as it pulls across the target line.

Weight shift: There must be a transfer of weight back to the left side from the right to prevent "falling away from" the hitting zone and to continue accelerating the clubhead through the ball. When the backswing reaches the "stop" position of the braced right foot, the forward movement of the swing is started by the body springing away from the inside of the foot. A natural transference of weight can occur only if the follow-through is unrestricted with the left foot open and receptive to a continuation of the swing.

In a free and unrestricted swing, the weight moves *to* the inside of the braced right foot where it is "caught" and held to allow the body to coil as far as possible. But when the weight transfers back to the left into the follow-through it rolls *across* the left foot. This enables the golfer to stay down and swing through the ball, extending the arms outward toward the target while still turning to complete the swing.

"Raising up" or "pulling up" on the shot causes "topping" and occurs when the hands hit up on the ball instead of through it—frequently as a

On a full follow-through the weight shifts to the left and rolls across the left foot.

result of hitting into a "square" left foot which stiffens the left leg and raises the hands at impact.

Distance is gained by letting the weight roll on *across* the left foot to extend the arms into the follow-through. If the left foot is closed, the left ankle and hip are unable to turn which restricts completing the swing. If the left foot is too far open, the clubhead is misdirected because the foot is rolling too far left, which prevents directing the clubhead toward the target. Positioning the feet approximately as described, with the left foot angled open in relationship to the right, promotes weight transference and coordination through the entire golf swing.

E: Determines width of stance: Positioning the feet the width of the shoulders provides strong stability for the swing and prevents momentum from forcing the body off-balance. Somewhat like an architectural column, strength and stability come from the width of the foundation being slightly greater than the width at the top.

Positioning the feet the width of the shoulders, then angling the feet outward, will angle the toes slightly beyond the shoulder line—the left foot more so than the right. Consequently, the actual width of the stance, in relationship to the shoulders, should be measured from the heels.

The width of the stance is determined by the club being used because the length of the shaft determines how large the swing arc will be. In turn, the arc of the swing determines how much momentum is generated

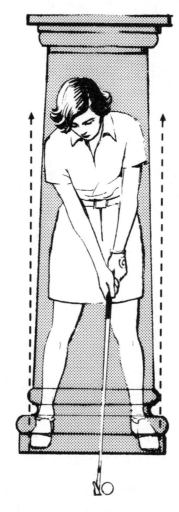

As an architectural column gains strength and stability from a base that is wider than the top, stability for the swing is maintained by extending the toes slightly beyond the width of the shoulders.

throughout the swing. The bigger the arc, the more momentum—and momentum affects balance.

Woods and longer irons with a big swing arc and maximum momentum need the wider stance, but short irons develop less momentum because the arc of the swing is somewhat smaller. Since momentum is less and balance can be maintained with the shorter swing radius, the stance can narrow with the short irons for more control and accuracy.

When using longer woods and irons, too narrow a stance will not provide stability for the body to maintain balance. In a natural effort to maintain balance, there is a tendency to "hunch up" the shoulders—to make the width of the shoulders *feel* equal to the width of the feet—which cramps and restricts the swing. A stance too wide, however, creates a different problem. Good balance can be maintained and a firm foundation assured, but the joints lock and make it physically difficult to make a full hip and shoulder turn.

F: Positions ball correctly: The position of the ball between the feet moves forward or back along the line of flight with the use of different clubs; the hands move closer to the body as the shafts get shorter (which moves the line of flight in closer) and the stance narrows and sometimes opens slightly with the use of shorter irons.

When the ball is positioned accurately, it is positioned between and away from the feet at a point where each golf club will contact the ball squarely in the center of the clubface, right at the bottom of the swing (rather than on the downswing or upswing, or on the heel or toe, which results in mis-hitting the shot). The difference between a mis-hit shot and a solid connection, however, is not always a matter of inches and many of these shots are quite close to perfection. Consistently hitting a little behind or on top of the ball or a little off-center on the clubface is frequently corrected just by positioning the ball more carefully in relationship to the feet.

The ball is played as far forward as the left instep with the use of the driver, graduating back down toward the center of the stance and closer to the feet as the shafts get shorter and the loft of the club increases. Although no one can determine with any authority exactly where "the spot" should be to comfortably fit each individual swing with the use of different clubs, there are guidelines and procedures to follow to help all golfers establish their own correct positions.

Many golfers encounter difficulty in positioning the ball correctly and making accurate alignments simply because they have no guidelines to follow. Following a fundamentally exact routine for establishing the position of address, however, helps each golfer consistently position the ball correctly with the use of every club. The routine should include (1) assuming the left hand grip; (2) standing upright with the feet together;

(3) extending the left arm in a straight arm-shaft position; (4) soling the clubhead squarely on the ground directly behind the ball and square to the target; (5) squaring the feet to the clubface; then (6) *separating the feet from the clubhead rather than from the ball.* Learning the procedure with the five iron, which is being used for instructional purposes, makes it easier to position the ball more accurately with all of the other clubs. The procedure is the same.

The five iron is a key middle club in the set of clubs and is centered between the feet in the basic golf swing. Although the ball is positioned differently with the use of different clubs, establishing an accurate bottom-of-the-swing position for the five iron also establishes a base position and basic standard procedure which golfers can use to position the ball correctly for all golf shots.

Before proceeding with club and ball alignment, the following diagram explains general club selection and where the ball is played in relationship to the feet with the use of different clubs:

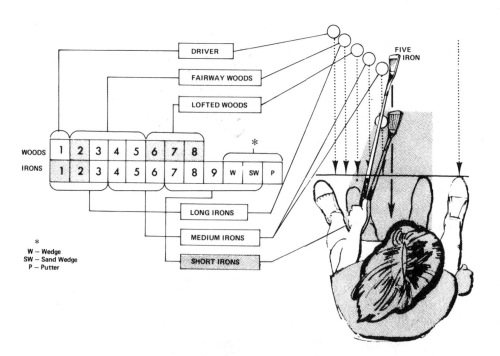

The rules of golf, which are governed by the United States States Golf Association and the Royal and Ancient Golf Club of St. Andrews, Scotland, allow each player a maximum of fourteen clubs, including the putter. The boxes in the diagram represent the choice of clubs available from which each golfer may select the fourteen clubs which "fit" his own golf game. The shaded numbers represent the clubs that are most frequently excluded from the set, by preference, either because they are difficult to play or because they are "special" lofted woods which replace both long and medium irons.

When learning to position the ball correctly many unnecessary difficulties can be avoided by first learning a procedure for positioning the clubhead accurately in relationship to the feet as well as to the ball. Once the procedure is developed positioning the ball correctly is much more automatic and far less difficult.

In the preceding chapter, the edge of the five iron was soled on the string where the two strings cross. Separating the feet from the clubhead to the width of the shoulders, centering the clubhead between the heels, will position the ball forward of center where the five iron will contact it squarely at the bottom of the swing:

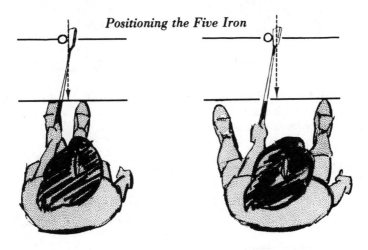

Positioning the Five Iron

Separating the feet from the clubhead, centering the clubhead between the heels, accurately positions the ball forward of center from the five iron through the wedge.

Positioning the ball correctly prevents a subconscious tendency to either "fall away from" or "lunge through" a ball positioned too far right or too far forward. For instance, separating the feet from the ball rather than from the clubhead *by not soling the clubhead first* generally positions the ball toward the right foot. Although a good setup for an intentional "punch" shot, normally on the downswing the clubhead either hits the top of the ball by contacting the ball before reaching the bottom of the swing, or pushes or slices to the right by hitting the ball before the clubface is square. More often, however, in a subconscious effort to adjust the swing to the ball position, rather than the weight shifting left on the downswing the body pulls away from the ball, either topping the ball by "skulling" it on the upswing or hitting the ground behind the ball by "falling away" on the downswing.

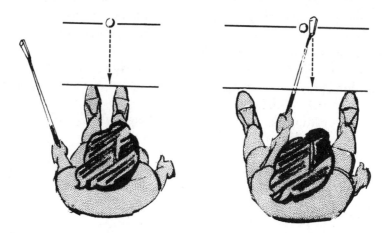

Separating the feet from the ball rather than from the clubhead (by not positioning the clubhead first) causes topping by positioning the clubhead too far back in the stance.

It is important to sole the clubhead *directly behind* the ball at address to position the ball correctly. Although the feet and clubhead may be accurate, a casual placement of the clubhead several inches behind the ball positions the ball too far forward. The clubhead either hits a "fat"

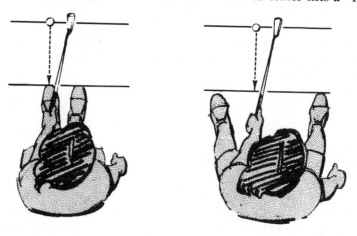

A casual placement of the clubhead several inches behind the ball at address positions the ball too far forward.

golf shot by reaching the bottom of the swing and the ground before contacting the ball, or tops the ball by catching it on the upswing. In an effort to make square contact, the body may lunge forward toward the ball and block the follow-through.

Positioning the driver: Before positioning the driver or the fairway woods it is important to note that although the same procedure is used for positioning the woods as is used for the irons, the clubhead will not lie flat on the ground until the position of address is completed. The back edge of the woods will be slightly off the ground until additional fundamentals establish a "sitting down" position.

The long shaft and shallow face of the driver makes it difficult to contact the ball at the bottom of the swing unless the ball is positioned as

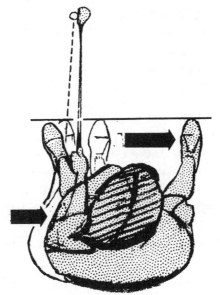

Positioning the driver. Stepping forward only slightly, aligning the left heel to the clubface, positions the ball off the left instep. Moving the right foot to the width of the shoulders then moves the body to the right to establish the driving stance.

far forward as the left heel. Consequently, the left foot barely steps forward to make an accurate alignment. Placing the left heel in line with the clubface positions the ball off the left instep. Moving the right foot to the width of the shoulders then moves the entire body right—without changing other established positions—and automatically establishes an accurate driving stance.

Positioning the fairway woods and long irons: Although the fairway woods and long irons are not positioned as far forward as the driver, they are still positioned forward toward the left heel. Using the same procedure for positioning the driver, position the longer woods and irons merely by stepping forward a *little* farther with the left foot before positioning the right.

Positioning the medium irons: Medium irons refer to the four and six as well as to the five, but the four iron should be considered the last of the long iron set and played forward of the center of the stance. Although the six iron is positioned the same as the five—in the center of the stance—it is also the first of the short iron set where the stance may start to narrow.

Positioning the lofted woods: Lofted woods are "specialty" clubs which replace both long and medium irons. Because of the lofted clubface many golfers find them easier to use, particularly where loft and "carry" as well as distance are equally as important. They are generally positioned the same or, because of the longer shafts, slightly forward of the irons they replace.

Positioning the short irons: Below the five iron is a game within a game where precision and accuracy are paramount to distance. All of the woods and irons, from the driver through the five iron, are positioned with a square stance and square hips with the feet the width of the shoulders as a strong foundation for a full golf swing. Although the procedure for positioning the clubhead, feet, and ball is the same for shorter irons as for longer clubs, the hands are progressively closer to the body with the shorter shafts which calls for altering the stance somewhat.

Narrowing the stance: As the hands move closer to the body with the use of shorter clubs, the swing becomes more upright and the arc of the swing much smaller, whereupon better control and balance are obtained by narrowing the stance. The shorter the shaft, the narrower the stance should be. Consequently, the feet are separated well within the shoulder line, narrowing even more with the use of shorter clubs.

Opening the stance: Along with narrowing the stance, opening the stance for short irons restricts a full hip turn, shortens the backswing, and produces more accuracy. Understanding open stance positions helps position the feet more accurately.

Short irons are unique from other clubs. Not only are they used to obtain their own maximum distance as with other irons, but they are also used for an unlimited variety of short shots to the green. The extreme versatility of short irons makes the placement of the feet somewhat difficult to understand because below the five iron the stance is adjusted, from square to open, according to the shot being made. Combined with this factor is the fact that golfers themselves are versatile in how they use open positions. As a result, the use of open stance positions must be determined by personal experimentation and results, not by what other golfers do. It can only be determined by understanding the purpose of opening the stance and then practicing and comparing square and open positions.

A position of address has been established with the feet aligned squarely to the line of flight but with the *angle* of the left foot open in relationship to the right—and the square position of the hips has been protected by the sequence in which fundamentals have been presented. An open stance is obtained by stepping forward with the left foot but placing the left foot from one to four inches short of the directional line, which is now maintained by the square position of the hips. The right foot is then positioned an equal distance to the right with the toes of the right foot on the directional line, aligned to the line of flight. The *angle* of the feet is the same as with other clubs.

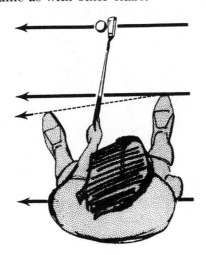

An open stance is obtained by placing the left foot one to four inches short of the directional line, then moving the right foot onto the directional line—which is now maintained by the square position of the hips.

Opening the stance with the feet while keeping the hips square restricts a full pivot which, in effect, turns a full golf swing into a smaller golf swing by shortening the length of the backswing. With the hands in close, the swing is upright and more hand control and accuracy is obtained with a shorter backswing.

Forcing additional distance with short iron shots changes timing and rhythm and invariably pulls the ball left. For that matter, pulling also

Consistency and accuracy develop by learning to make the backswing

occurs as a result of applying *maximum* hitting power to any golf shot. Rather than "pressing" for maximum distance and "leaning on" a wedge, for instance, more control and accuracy is obtained by opening the stance just slightly to shorten the backswing and using the same "grooved" swing to hit a smooth nine iron instead.

The key to using open stance positions is in learning how much to open the stance to regulate the length of the backswing for the shot being made, for the backswing and follow-through are equally the same, from the driver through the wedge, from full golf shots with all golf clubs to short shots to the green. "Quitting on" the short shots, or stopping at the ball, is always a result of swinging back too far. This prevents being *able*

and follow-through equally the same from the driver through the wedge.

to hit and follow through. The length of the backswing is determined by the length of the shot. The shorter the shot being played the more open the stance should be to help minimize the backswing movement. Confidence develops in *hitting* short shots only by shortening the backswing in order to be *able* to follow through at least the same distance as the backswing movement.

A completely open stance is used for short pitch or chip shots, moving more toward square for longer distances. Whatever the distance, however, the feet are separated initially for that particular shot as determined by practicing different setups and practicing the follow-through with a shortened backswing. "Sense and feel," which are so important to this phase of the game, can only be developed through experimentation and practice.

Since the arc of the swing is shorter with the shorter irons, many experienced golfers also advocate opening the hips at address along with opening the stance with the feet, theorizing that this simply gets the left hip out of the way *before* the backswing starts. This precise kind of accuracy, however, should be predicated on the needs and experience of individual golfers. With the exception of possibly very short shots, opening the hips along with the feet is not necessarily a good procedure for less-than-experienced golfers.

The directional line of the feet and hips is part of the target line and when the stance is open at address, square hips maintain the directional line. With the clubface square and the hips open too, however, the directional line is no longer parallel to the line of flight, which then alters the target line. The tendency is to push the clubhead back on the angled *directional* line but *outside* the line of flight, whereupon either the swing pattern changes to "loop" the clubhead back to the line of flight or the clubhead returns to cut across the ball by cutting across the target lines. Used effectively and intentionally by experts who swing from "outside-in" with an open clubface to hit high "cut shots," opening the hips along with the feet and "cutting across" the ball can be hazardous for less experienced golfers until they become expert with the basic shots.

Opening the stance with the feet and keeping the hips square for short shots still shortens the backswing for control but will start the clubhead on the line of flight as it follows the line of the hips. Golfers who still prefer to open the hips, however, should first square the clubface, then consciously *start* the clubhead back on the line of flight unless they are *intentionally* practicing high "cut" shots with an open clubface (which, incidentally, unless practiced to perfection, may lead to shanking the ball as well).

The same kind of accuracy essential to experienced golfers who combine open feet and hip positions to finesse and manipulate the ball does not necessarily have to be obtained by average golfers. They might do better using a familiar, comfortably square position of the hips to make certain they are somewhere on the green and putting. It minimizes an effort toward perfection, which is apt to dump the ball in a bunker or land it short of the green rather than two feet from the hole. On *full* short iron shots, even experienced golfers may keep the hips square—and frequently the feet as well. Many retain the square hip position even for short shots to the green.

Although perfection is for experts, once golfers become proficient in using square positions, some consideration and experimentation should be given to opening the stance with short irons because proficiency continues to develop through knowledge, experimentation, and practice. Experimentation should be done by first playing full short iron shots from a completely square position, then adjusting only the feet, before opening the hips along with the feet, to play the same golf shot. Tiny adjustments in the stance make big differences in the swing and are reflected in results. Proceeding slowly, an inch at a time, combined with experimental practice, enables golfers to quickly determine for themselves how much "control" is beneficial to their own short game.

Distribution of weight: As the stance begins to narrow with the use of shorter irons, establishing the weight progressively more toward the left promotes better hand action and more control with less weight shift and a minimal body turn. Establishing the weight toward the left helps position the hands well forward at address, helping the hands return ahead of the ball and guide the ball toward the target with stronger action of the hands and arms.

When using longer woods and irons, before the stance begins to narrow, the weight is equally distributed between the feet. By the time the stance is narrowed to where the nine or wedge is used, however, the weight should be more firmly toward the left and toward the heels for balance.

Summary on separating the feet and playing the short irons: When learning to play the short irons, the procedure for positioning the clubhead is the same as for other clubs: squaring the clubface to the target with a straight left arm, feet together, and stance erect. The feet are then separated according to the shot being played, taking into consideration that the stance narrows and opens with the use of different clubs and the weight moves progressively toward the left as the shafts get shorter.

The following two chapters complete the position of address by "sitting down to the ball" before completing the grip and finalizes the important step-by-step procedure for setting up to the ball. With practice, golfers will learn to quickly assess the shot, step up to the ball, *accurately* position the feet, make minor adjustments and *confidently* play the shot. Concentrating on making the backswing and follow-through equally the same puts the same golf swing on the shorter shots as on the longer shots, from a full golf swing with square positions to a miniature half or "soft" three-quarter swing with a fully open stance.

10

Fundamental #6—Flexing the Knees in Toward Each Other

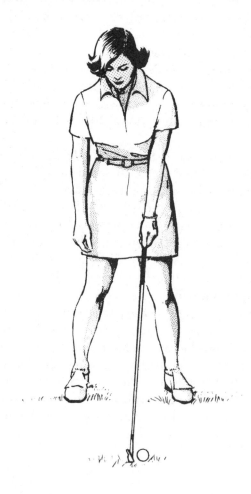

A single position has been established up to this point which will be influenced in different ways as the knees flex toward each other. Some positions have been established for the *purpose* of being changed to establish new positions. For this reason, it is important to rebuild the address position which precedes this movement in the manner in which fundamentals have been presented.

As the knees flex inward the entire lower body, left arm, hand, and club will be accurately positioned as the final stage in positioning the lower body. Meanwhile, other established positions remain unchanged.

How to Achieve Fundamental #6:

"Release" the tucked-in hip position by extending the hips slightly

"Sitting down to the ball."

backward and "sticking the seat out a bit." Along with the action flex the knees *inward* by flexing them toward each other. As the body lowers, let the left hand move slightly down and inward. Although all of the movements are very slight, accuracy results from flexing the knees inward rather than bending the knees forward.

Purposes:

A. Maintains an upright stance and good balance by "sitting down to the ball."
B. Establishes accurate position of left hand at address.
C. Completes weight distribution between and on the feet.
D. Relaxes but strengthens the legs.

A: Maintains an upright stance and good balance by "sitting down to the ball:" "Sitting down to the ball" is an expression used in golf for lowering the body from the knees into a somewhat "sitting down" position by "sticking the seat out a bit" as the knees flex inward. The reasons for doing so should be self-evident from the moment the position is established. While "dropping" the left hand into an accurate position

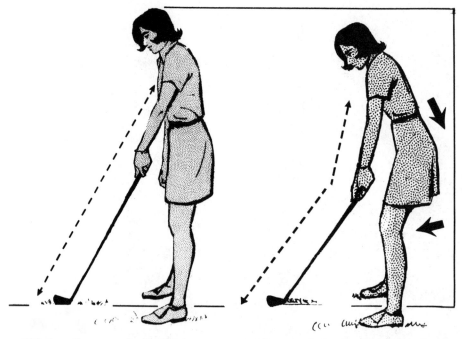

"Sitting down to the ball" is an expression used for lowering the body from the knees into a somewhat "sitting down" position while maintaining an upright stance.

and maintaining balance, the feet and legs instantly cock into a strong feeling of action as the entire lower body gets set to move powerfully and actively back through the ball.

"Sitting down to the ball" is a very slight, almost imperceptible movement (but critical movements in golf are frequently very slight). Lowering the body too far downward, beyond "unlocking" the knees, generally causes "chopping" back at the ball and hitting behind the ball as the body pulls up through the backswing and lowers rather dramatically coming back to the ball. Topping occurs, however, when the body stays down through the backswing but pulls up through the ball.

Lowering the body from the knees keeps the stance upright and prevents the weight from slipping forward while positioning the clubhead. As the knees flex inward they also bend forward, and sticking the seat out a bit maintains balance by counteracting the forward knee movement.

B: Establishes accurate position of left hand at address: Standing upright and flexing the knees in toward each other forces the left arm to compensate by moving the left hand down and inward as the body lowers approximately two inches. This "sitting down" position soles the driver and fairway woods flat on the ground as the hand drops down.

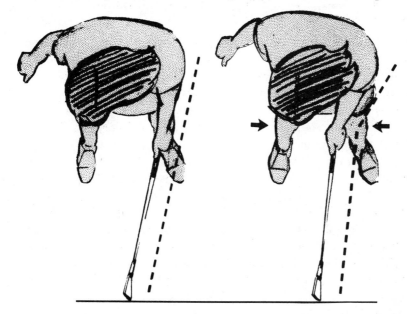

Lowering the body from the knees changes the straight arm-shaft position (left), accurately positioning the left hand at address by lowering and moving the left hand slightly down and inward (right).

The repositioned left hand, moving closer to the right, makes it easier to keep the hips square while completing the grip. Although the angle of the wrist will change, other positions remain unchanged. The position of the clubhead will remain the same, with the clubface square to the line of flight and the left hand still ahead of the ball.

Letting the left hand move down and inward changes the angle of the left wrist from straight to bent, as seen from both the top and side. The bent *downward* position promotes accurate hand action through the swing, and the bent *inward* position will enable the hands to press forward to get a "running start" on the backswing. Completing the grip will not change these positions.

C: Completes exact weight distribution between and on the feet: Sticking the seat out a bit as the knees flex inward lowers the body straight downward and moves a small amount of weight off the heels toward the balls of the feet. The "sitting down" position protects weight distribution which has been established up to this point by preventing the weight from slipping forward onto the toes and keeping the weight distributed between the feet rather than shifting left or right. Flexing the knees in toward each other completes accurate weight distribution at address by putting the weight inside the feet.

Equal weight distribution between the feet and a balanced position at address helps transfer weight while swinging, but shifting the weight to the *inside* of the feet turns on the power system by tensing and strengthening the upper inside leg muscles, reinforcing the foundation of the swing and putting "feeling" in the feet. Along with a fairly closed angle of the right foot at address, establishing and keeping the weight inside the foot further prevents the weight from rolling across the right foot on the backswing as the weight shifts to the right. Rhythm, timing, and good footwork are promoted by flexing the knees inward. Swaying is prevented as the shoulders and hips turn *against* the strong right foot position, which prevents a lateral movement. At the top of the swing the weight shifts left as the action of the swing pushes against the *inside* of the foot rather than staying on the right or shifting farther right by pushing against the *outside* of the foot.

Accurate weight distribution at address is one of the more sensitive feelings in golf which is more readily obtained by applying fundamentals in sequence. Even then, however, weight distribution may change somewhat while setting up to the ball. A sudden weight shift either left or right is indicated by one knee jutting forward ahead of the other by *placing* the weight on that side. Jutting one knee ahead of the other—which is more apt to occur to the left—sets up poor leg movement. The knees continue to jut and dip throughout the golf swing, changing the arc of the swing by lowering and raising the body and lessening the odds of returning the clubhead accurately.

The overall feeling of accurate weight distribution at address is somewhat similar to that of a boxer's stance, coupled with a feeling of being able to spring straight upward from the position.

D: Relaxes but strengthens the legs: Strength is created by tensing the inside thigh muscles of the legs as the weight moves to the inside of the feet. But even as the muscles are tensed to produce power, at the same time the legs must be relaxed and supple to promote a smooth and fluid swing. This is not a contradiction, in that strength and relaxation are obtained simultaneously when the knees turn inward because they *cannot* turn inward to strengthen the muscles without extending forward to relax the legs.

Strength results from flexing the muscles, but good footwork and relaxed and supple legs result from unlocking the knee joints rather than standing stiff-legged. The legs can then swing both left and right in a natural swinging movement. The difference can quickly be determined simply by swinging the arms around with the knees first stiff, then flexed.

11

Fundamental #7—Placing the Right Hand on the Club

So much emphasis has been placed on addressing the ball with just the left hand grip that there is reason to question, by now, why every golfer who plays the game is generally observed to address the ball with the grip already completed. First of all, there are two varieties of golfers involved: those who already apply fundamentals and those who don't; the proficient and the inexperienced.

Proficient golfers establish the position of address by familiarity and "feel," personalizing the position but doing so with accuracy through understanding. Although the hands are on the club together, it is almost certain that the right hand is loosely placed—in effect still *off* the club—until *after* positions are secured. The larger percentage of inexperienced golfers approach the ball with a firm, two-handed grip and inadvertently proceed to establish positions incorrectly. Although all golfers eventually develop a stylized system for addressing the ball, proficiency evolves through understanding the concepts of the swing. Once understood, the position of address can be established even by initiating the procedure with a completed grip.

Addressing the ball with the grip completed prevents an opportunity to use the hands independently to obtain specific objectives. While the left hand is used to establish positions, the right hand is off the club to prevent muscles activated by the use of the right arm from interfering with positions being established. Positioning the right hand, however, just as positioning the left, obtains objectives of its own. As the grip is completed, it will become apparent that withholding the right hand from the club until the knees are flexed is a contributing factor in continuing to establish accurate positions.

How to Achieve Fundamental #7:

Based on prior fundamentals, rebuild positions as they have been established up to this point. Be *particularly* careful not to disturb the square position of the hips or weight distribution and simply extend the right hand to complete the grip. Keep the shoulders relaxed and let the right shoulder move naturally downward.

Purposes:

A. Protects square position of the hips.
B. Positions the shoulders while completing the grip.
C. Completes an upright, balanced position.

A: Protects square position of the hips: One of the more difficult positions for golfers to establish and maintain at address is the square position of the hips, which are easily influenced to slip into an open position. A specific reason for building the position of address without the grip completed is to make absolutely certain that the square hip position, once established, is protected.

The hips easily establish or slip into an open position at address *unless* the knees are flexed and the body is in a "sitting down" position *before* the grip is secured. Review for a moment the position of address established before "sitting down to the ball." With the stance upright, legs straight, and the feet separated, the right hand must move several inches downward to the left in order to complete the grip. Keep the legs straight and simulate placing the right hand on the club by barely starting the right hand diagonally downward toward the left. The *moment* the movement starts, the hips coordinate with the muscular movement of the right arm and move into an open position.

Lowering the body into the "sitting down" position *before* placing the right hand on the club overcomes the muscular influence the right arm

Moving the right arm diagonally downward to complete the grip before "sitting down to the ball" forces the hips into an open position.

has on the movement of the hips. The left arm, though still extended, moves the left hand closer to the right, eliminating some of the muscular conflict by minimizing the distance the right hand would otherwise have to extend diagonally downward. The knee joints, unlocked by the flexing movement, relieve muscular tension which causes muscular conflict between the right arm and the hips. At this point, the right hand is almost in position to complete the grip and muscular movement is less apt to push the hips open.

Although sitting down to the ball removes most of the muscular conflict, the short distance the right hand has yet to extend will *still* influence the hips unless mental awareness protects the hip position. Knowing how easily the hips slide open, however, helps keep them in place and square to the line of flight.

B: Positions the shoulders while completing the grip: The shoulders are not a factor, along with the feet and hips, in establishing the directional line. They are positioned by other fundamentals and there should be no effort made to position the shoulders in order to let them be positioned naturally. An accurate shoulder position is established, however, by (1) positioning the clubhead with the left shoulder forward; (2) flexing the knees; (3) keeping the hips square at address; and (4) letting the right shoulder drop lower than the left when the right hand completes the grip.

Preventing the extended left arm and square hips from changing position as the right hand completes the grip positions the shoulders, along with the hips, square to the line of flight. The right shoulder is naturally positioned lower than the left, simply because the right hand is lower than the left when the grip is complete. Square shoulders, with the right shoulder lower than the left, position the shoulders to turn naturally through the swing. This makes it easier to swing through the ball, toward the target, *on* the target line.

The shoulder turn is not something that should be controlled or maneuvered because it complicates and disturbs rhythm and timing in the swing by overemphasizing the action. The shoulders and hips are positioned square at address to coordinate and turn with the movement of the left arm pushing the clubhead through the backswing. An accurate shoulder turn is only an indication that other fundamentals which *produce* a natural shoulder turn and pivot have been applied correctly.

Some controversy occasionally develops over whether the address position of the shoulders should be slightly open as opposed to square. It is helpful to remember, however, that *naturally* assumed positions can better coordinate with other fundamentals and, also, that positions

Positioning the Shoulders

Front View   Top View

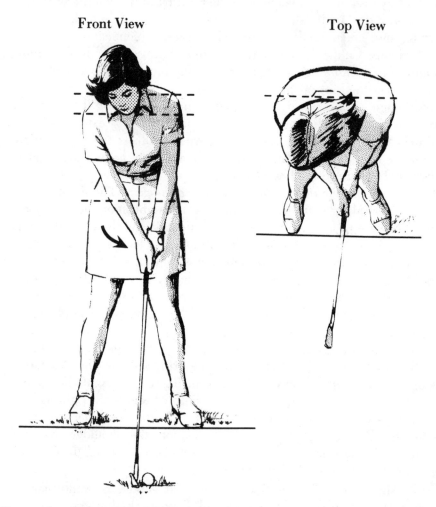

Preventing the extended left arm and square hips from moving while positioning the right hand draws the right shoulder down lower than the left while keeping the shoulders "square"—squaring all positions to the line of flight.

naturally seek to return to the approximate same position assumed at address. A square, canted shoulder position at address (aside from being natural) places the left shoulder to turn under the chin *with* the initial backswing movement. The right shoulder, out of the way and ready to turn, is positioned to come back around and under from the top of the swing in an effort to return to the same address position—the natural shoulder movement in a natural golf swing.

Square shoulders at address, with the right shoulder lower than the left, brings the right shoulder back and under on the downswing in a natural effort to return to the same address position.

C: Completes an upright, balanced position: An upright stance and balanced position at address promotes a balanced, upright swing. A common practice, however, is to step up to the ball with the grip completed and the legs straight, lean over too far to position the clubhead, and establish the weight on the toes. From such a position, it is difficult to either swing comfortably, naturally or accurately.

The sequence in which fundamentals are presented establish and protect both the upright stance and weight distribution by positioning the clubhead with just the left hand while standing upright, then flexing the knees and lowering the body straight down to secure positions *before* extending the right arm to complete the grip. The "sitting down" position of the lower body maintains a balanced, upright stance and equal weight distribution as the upper body leans forward only enough to complete the grip. With practice, once the procedure is developed setting up to the ball correctly will become a quick, comfortable, and accurate routine—*even* with a completed grip.

12

Fundamental #8—Rolling the Elbows In

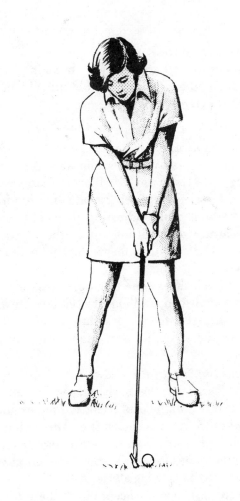

The final movement in establishing the position of address is rolling the elbows inward toward each other. Firmly securing positions a fraction of a second before the backswing starts "triggers" the backswing movement.

How to Achieve Fundamental #8:

Rebuild the position of address, then roll the elbows toward each other to *firm* the left arm. As the inside of the elbows roll upward and the arms move clother together, position the right arm slightly lower than the left and a little more relaxed. Relaxing the right arm also has a tendency to relax the right hand grip, so make certain the grip stays firm.

Purposes:

A. Avoids tension at address.
B. Firmly positions the left arm to resist "breaking" on the backswing.
C. Loosely positions the right arm to fold quickly on the backswing.
D. Locks in a full extension of the arms.

A: Avoids tension at address: Rolling the elbows toward each other as a final movement at address avoids tension at address and *through* the swing by keeping the arms relaxed while positions are established. A certain amount of looseness and relaxation is needed for a comfortable interlocking of positions while adjusting them to each other. A rigid extension of the arms while setting up to the ball creates muscular tension, making it difficult to either establish a relaxed position or produce a relaxed, fluid swing.

Setting up to the ball takes time to adjust positions. When positions are comfortably established, rolling the elbows inward just as the backswing starts strengthens muscles throughout the body with just enough tension for the swinging movement while avoiding too much tension at address.

B: Firmly positions the left arm to resist "breaking" on the backswing: A golfer quickly learns in the early stages of the game to avoid compulsive golf lessons from helpful friends or fellow golfers by keeping the left arm straight through the backswing. Although the advice should be taken well, neither friendly help nor self-determination will keep the left arm straight unless the elbows are rolled inward at address with the left arm firm *before* the backswing starts. A firm left arm at address and through the backswing promotes accuracy at the top of the swing by completing the shoulder turn—and accuracy at the top of the swing promotes accuracy at impact.

The left arm and shaft should be thought of as one long rod, hinged only in the middle by the wrist which "breaks" naturally through the backswing. If this rod is allowed to have two hinges, at both the wrist *and* the elbow by "bowing" the elbow outward at address, the golfer swings into a floppy, loose entanglement at the top of the swing which will preclude any ability of the left side to maintain control. Only an inept slapping at the ball results. The hands pick up the club on the backswing, throw it from the top, and straight down into the ground directly behind the ball. This chopping motion destroys the swing and should be reserved for felling trees, not playing golf.

To demonstrate the importance of rolling the elbows in, extend the left arm without rolling the elbow in (A) and pull against the left wrist with the right hand (B). The arm easily "gives" because the elbow bends. With the inside of the elbow facing upward, however (C), the arm is strongly braced against the pull and keeps the left arm straight (D).

Pulling against the left arm is only a small indication of the force exerted on the elbow by momentum through the backswing. It is physically difficult for the arm to resist such additional force unless the left elbow is first rolled inward and the arm firmly positioned before the backswing starts.

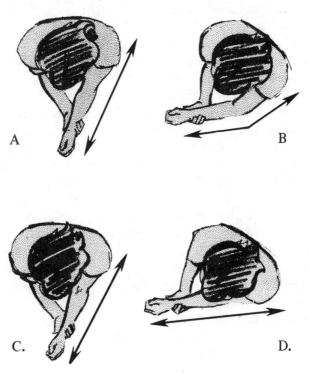

Testing left arm firmness.

When rolling the elbows toward each other, it should be remembered that positions must be accurate but they must not be overestablished. Forcing the elbows in *too* tightly restricts a comfortable swinging movement by preventing muscles from continuing to contract through the backswing. The same test above can be used to determine how *much* the elbows should be rolled inward to maintain firmness without locking the elbow joints or causing tension by stretching the arms too tightly.

C: Loosely positions the right arm to fold quickly on the backswing: Rolling the elbows toward each other affects the two arms differently. Although firming the left arm prevents it from "breaking" through the backswing, loosely positioning the right arm slightly lower than the left helps the right arm fold with the elbow pointing down rather than "flying" upward through the backswing. Along with loosely positioning the arm, however, there is also a tendency to loosen the right hand, and caution must be exercised to firm the grip as the backswing starts. Firming the grip puts a certain amount of relaxed firmness back in the right arm, strengthening both arms at address.

Control is maintained through the backswing by the firm left arm so there is no danger of the clubhead going out of control if the right arm is relaxed. To the contrary, the right arm position helps keep the elbow down to wedge the clubhead through the right swing pattern. Extending the right arm the same as the left positions the right arm higher and prevents this natural action.

D: Locks in a full extension of the arms: A full extension of the arms throughout the golf swing maintains the swing radius for a maximum swing arc. The arms are fully extended *together*, however, at only one point. Just beyond impact the muscles of both arms are fully extended as the extension of the left arm passes naturally to the right.

Keeping the arms relaxed to establish positions, but rolling the elbows in as the backswing starts, strengthens and enables the left arm to extend through the backswing. Although the right arm is relaxed and not extended at address, hitting through the ball extends the right arm into the follow-through. Rolling the elbows in as the backswing starts "locks in" this full extension by positioning the arms correctly.

Positions want to return to the same position they established at the start of the swing. Rolling the elbows inward keeps the right elbow down and the right arm passive through the backswing. When the right arm returns with the elbow down, the arm extends through the ball rather than weakening and folding as the left arm folds in the follow-through.

BUILDING
THE POSITION OF ADDRESS

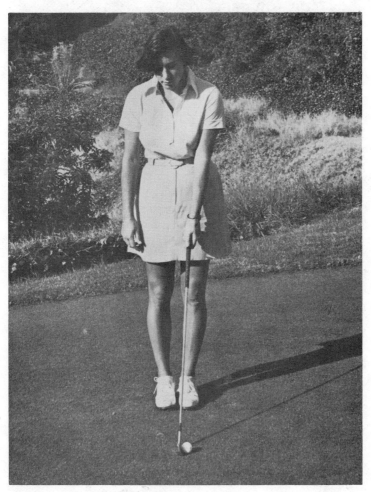

Positioning the clubhead.

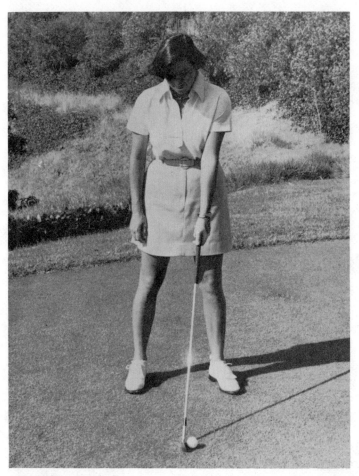

Separating the feet.

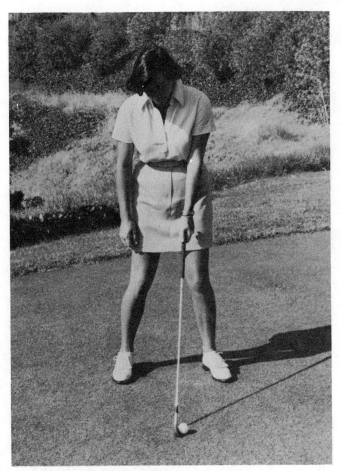

Flexing the knees in toward each other.

Placing the right hand on the club.

Rolling the elbows in.

13

The "Waggle"

Many pages have been devoted to establishing the position of address, but the position itself, as a whole, is established in a matter of seconds. Quickly and confidently addressing the ball is a matter of understanding objectives, establishing exact positions, and smoothing positions together into a coordinated relationship with each other by learning to use the "waggle." Learning to waggle is the key to starting a rhythmical, repeating pattern for a smooth, coordinated swing, but the purpose of waggling is difficult to understand unless positions are established in sequence along with a knowledgeable application of the use of fundamentals.

The purpose of waggling is three-fold: (1) to develop consistency and rhythm at address and through the swing by following an exact routine for establishing and coordinating positions with continuous rhythmical movement; (2) to replace conscious thought through the swing with concentration at address by planning ahead for an overall action or result of the swing; and (3) to obtain objectives automatically in order to develop rhythm and concentration.

Addressing the ball with rhythm starts a rhythmical swing from the moment the clubhead is soled on the ground. As positions are established, a continous, rhythmical movement of feet, knees, hips, hands, and arms coordinate with a rhythmical movement of the clubhead to slightly overlap and adjust fundamental positions until objectives are obtained. Overall objectives, such as a square position of address, upright stance, balance, weight distribution, ball position, and accurate target line are obtained simultaneously along with primary objectives of independent positions by applying fundamentals in sequence with continuous movement. With practice, golfers instinctively become familiar with the feeling of coordination and accuracy and automatically roll the elbows in as a final *waggle* procedure to continue the movement of the swing.

Waggling quickly blends specific fundamental positions into one continuous movement by feel and reflex action, establishing and keeping positions "waggled" in place until the backswing starts of its own accord. When the swing starts automatically, thinking can then be directed toward an overall action or result of the swing, thereby overcoming conscious thought while swinging by applying concentration at address.

Although similar in definition, conscious thought and concentration affect the golf swing differently. Conscious thought is "mental awareness," generally directed toward specific positions or movements with deliberate thought and application. Although usually present at address to establish exact positions, a quick application of any conscious thought after the swing is underway may overemphasize some independent action during the swinging process which changes timing and rhythm. On the other hand, concentration replaces conscious thought while setting up to the ball either by (1) planning ahead for overall action or (2) planning the application of one "key thought."

Concentrating on overall action such as hitting through the ball or completing the follow-through, or concentrating on one key thought found to "trigger" an accurate swinging movement such as pushing into and against a braced right foot, *prevents* conscious thought while swinging and starts and maintains a smooth golf swing by *excluding* other thoughts.

Just as the swing itself is developed through practice, concentration develops by *practicing* concentration while establishing positions. The more proficient and experienced a golfer becomes, the less conscious thought is needed in setting up to the ball, the sooner concentration can be applied, and the less opportunity conscious thought has to affect the swinging movement.

The conscious mind is subconsciously motivated to emphasize anything, anywhere, not "programmed" in the waggle. Planning ahead for an overall result or action of the swing, however, emphasizes positions and movements *during* the waggle which are used throughout the swing to obtain a specific result—bringing to mind the old Scottish adage, "As ye waggle, so shall ye swing." Planning ahead is part of the waggle, and the waggle is part of the swing. When golfers waggle with a plan in mind, concentration and rhythm are much more likely to remain intact throughout the swinging movement.

Waggling is a "sense and feel" procedure which develops personal instinctive responses and concentration only through practice. By assuming each position independently, then speeding up the process, a natural ability develops for addressing the ball both quickly and automatically. Two types of waggles relate specifically to either positions or movements, and both are used with rhythmical application either separately or combined:

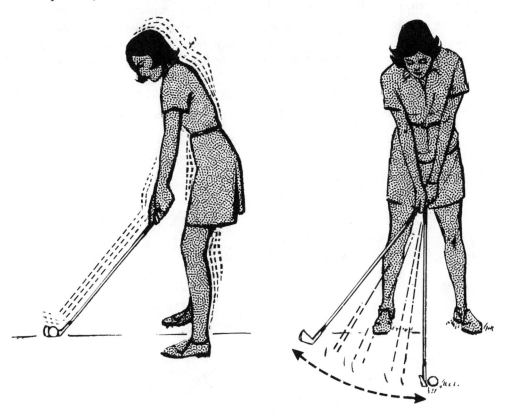

An up and down waggle (left) combined with a back-and-forth waggle (right) settles positions into place while rhythmically "feeling out" a good swing plan.

A slight up-and-down movement of the body and the clubhead establishes and coordinates body positions, particularly the lower body. This movement should be used initially to establish and keep positions waggled in place, particularly the square position of the hips which are easily influenced to change. As positions are established, concentration replaces conscious thought used in establishing positions with a back-and-forth movement of the clubhead behind the ball and on the line of flight to develop feeling for putting a good swing plan into effect.

Understanding and practicing each section of the swing, in this case addressing the ball with a waggle, grooves good habits and dispels a continuing concept in golf that too much thinking breeds "paralysis through analysis." An ability to waggle beneficially (as well as sensibly) is the result of understanding objectives by understanding the swing, otherwise it serves a somewhat meaningless purpose. Trusting fundamentals to attain specific objectives develops confidence in doing things instinctively, without paralysis of indecisive thought which stems from a lack of understanding. Once the position of address can be established systematically and quickly, golfers should experiment with personalizing the movement to find comfortable waggles of their own. Consistency in swinging the same way all the time begins at address by consistently setting up to the ball the same way every time.

Part 3
The Backswing "Push-Away"

14

Fundamental #9—The Forward Press

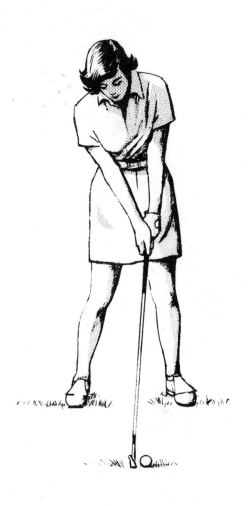

The forward press is a slight forward movement of the hands designed to accompany positions as they have been established up to this point. Although not all golfers use a forward press, fundamentals have been presented which employ its use because the advantages far outweigh the disadvantages of using a slight forward movement to start the movement of the backswing.

The forward press is not intended to dictate an absolute procedure for starting the backswing. It is important to develop a comfortable, individual system for applying fundamentals and golfers must determine for themselves whether to incorporate a forward movement into their own golf swing. Understanding the purpose of both the waggle and the forward press affords an opportunity to apply the principle involved whether or not the movement is used.

How to Achieve Fundamental #9:

As positions are waggled together and the elbows roll inward, push the butt of the right hand *down* and forward to push both hands into the straight arm-shaft position. Let the knees slide forward with the forward movement and be particularly careful to keep the hips and clubface square.

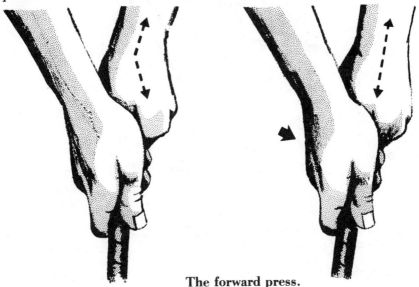

The forward press.

Purposes:

A. Determines the use of the forward press.

B.   Protects positions already established.
C.   Gets a "running start" on the backswing by putting the legs in motion.

A: Determines the use of the forward press: The purpose of the forward press is to move the hands forward into the originally established straight arm-shaft position, thereby straightening the left wrist and positioning the left arm to push the clubhead into the backswing rather than pulling the club back with the hands from a bent arm-shaft position. The factor which determines whether a golfer should use a forward press or not is whether the arm and shaft form one straight line as the backswing starts or whether the left wrist still bends inward.

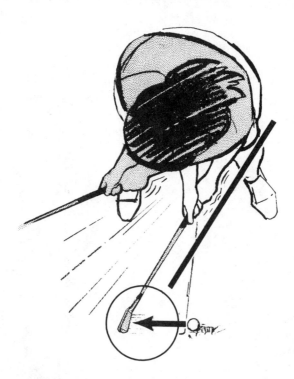

The purpose of the forward press is to straighten the left wrist so the clubhead can be pushed into the backswing with a firm left arm.

Pushing the clubhead into the backswing is a fundamental movement which turns the shoulders—and the shoulders turn the hips. Although the following chapter discusses the subject of pushing the clubhead back, the push position of the left arm is determined by either positioning the hands forward or by using the forward press or waggle.

The forward movement of the hands and the backward movement of the clubhead are each very distinctive but closely related to each other and to the waggle by timing. Because of this, many golfers either position or waggle the hands forward as opposed to a more independent movement of the hands pushing forward to start the backswing. When the hands are *positioned* forward while setting up to the ball, the backswing starts *from* the forward position rather than starting with a slight forward movement.

Although many golfers prefer to either establish or "waggle" into the straight arm-shaft position (determined by individual choice), positions can generally be established more accurately with the hands initially positioned more toward the center of the body. Also, positions can be waggled out of alignment while waggling into the forward position, which is more the tendency of the average golfer, and it is easier to start the backswing with a slight forward movement. Even experienced golfers use a forward press expressly for these reasons.

Building the swing originally positioned the left arm and shaft straight in line with each other, from which the left hand moved inward as the knees flexed toward each other. With the left wrist bent inward, however, particularly *too* far inward with the hands behind the ball, it is difficult to push the clubhead away from the ball because the hands are positioned to pull. "Taking" the club back from this position sets up a chain reaction which results in almost any form of poor golf shot,

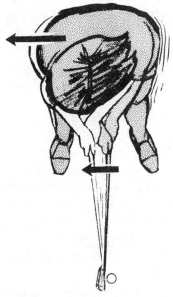

Starting the swing with the left wrist bent inward results in incorrect movements by positioning the hands to pull rather than push the clubhead away from the ball.

particularly the most awesome of all, the shank. Even the name brings fear to occasional shankers who avoid even the term by referring, instead, to "that lateral thing".

Shanking is caused by a series of incorrect movements which hits the ball straight right with an open clubface. With the left wrist bent inward, the hands pull the clubhead away from the ball with quick hand action and a fast backswing, moving the shoulders laterally by blocking the shoulder turn. These actions combine to whip the clubhead upward, loop the clubface open at the top of the swing, and whip the clubhead back to the ball with the face still open. As the weight shifts left with good lower body action, poor timing and coordination combined with a poor shoulder turn and late hand action prevent coming even close to squaring the clubface at impact. The result may be hitting the ball directly to the right by swinging "outside-in" and hitting the only available place on the wide open clubface, the crook—or shank—at the base of the shaft. "Toeing" the ball, however, which strongly resembles a shank, also occurs with this kind of action but stems from swinging "inside-out" and hitting on the toe of the open clubface.

Preventing problems is so much easier than finding and correcting them. Whipping the clubhead back and looping it at the top are faults which are easily prevented by using the forward press. The movement is frequently so slight as to be almost imperceptible.

The object of the forward press is to push the hands forward only so far as to reestablish the straight left arm-shaft position. Pressing the hands beyond that point "cock" the hands into pushing the clubhead upward which results in "picking up the clubhead." Although the movement almost invariably pushes the hips and clubface open, the result may be a low "punch" shot if the clubface stays square and returns in the same "hooded" position. (An *intentional* punch shot, however, positions the ball farther back rather than positioning the hands farther forward.) A very slight movement is more than sufficient when using the forward press.

B: Protects positions already established: Positions which are easily changed or may not be established accurately if the hands are either positioned *or* waggled forward are the square hips and clubface, equal distribution of weight between the feet, and the position of the hands. Both the waggle and the forward press protect these positions, however, by securing them *with* the waggle before pressing down and forward with the right hand.

Small, insignificant things are frequently overlooked in golf, such as how to use the forward press. Although an apparently trivial movement, pressing down and forward with the butt of the right hand pushes down on the handle and keeps the clubface square. At the same time, the

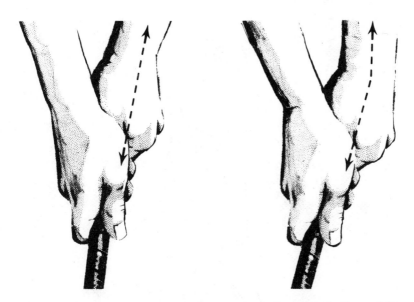

Pressing the hands too far beyond a straight arm-shaft position will either push the hips and clubface open and push the clubhead upward or "hood" a square clubface.

knees and hips slide forward and the weight rocks gently left, then right. Pressing both hands forward, or pulling the handle forward, pulls up on the handle and swings the clubface open. Preventing the clubface from swinging open also prevents the hands from moving upward out of an accurate position.

Along with protecting positions at address, the forward press makes certain the hands are ahead of the ball and positioned to push rather than pull the clubhead as the backswing starts.

C: Gets a "running start" on the backswing by putting the legs in motion: Getting a "running start" on the backswing gives impetus to the golf swing by starting the swing from a moving position. The waggle is generally given credit for being the connecting link between establishing positions and getting the backswing started, which is almost accurate because of the smooth coordination of the waggle and forward press. The backswing, however, starts with a slight "rocking forward" movement, and the influence the forward press has on the action of the knees starts the movement of the backswing by helping the knees slide forward to put the legs in motion.

Fundamental 7A in Chapter 11 explained how the movement of the right arm toward the left influenced the movement of the hips. With the body in a "sitting down" position and the knees flexed inward, this same muscular influence is exerted on the knees rather than on the hips. If

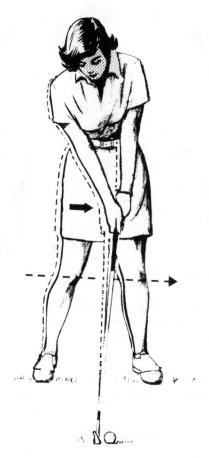

The forward press slides the knees toward the target, getting a "running start" on the backswing by putting the legs in motion. The movement, however, is very slight and the knees remain parallel to each other and to the line of flight.

positions have been established accurately, as the hands press forward the knees slide forward, changing location a degree or so, but not the parallel relationship of the knees to each other. A line in front of the knees would be parallel to the line of flight, rather than one knee jutting forward slightly ahead of the other.

The knees should be encouraged to become a natural part of the forward press. The movements are so closely related that even experienced golfers who profess to not using a forward press, per se, may indicate they start the swing in motion by pressing the right knee forward. Here again, experience and "feel" are important, but pressing the right knee forward as opposed to using the forward press has a tendency to dip the right knee forward and dip the left knee back.

Although the movement of the hands and knees are certainly simpatico, pressing the right knee forward does not always obtain the same results as letting the knees move with the movement of the hands.

The sliding movement of the knees is slight and very subtle and, like other swing movements, must not and need not be exaggerated. A very slight forward movement is enough to start a rhythmical, swinging movement while "cocking" the left leg toward the target and securing the weight more firmly on the inside of the right foot. With the weight equally distributed at address, the forward movement rocks the weight to the left and *back* to the right, which is the natural beginning of a correct weight shift.

Good footwork and coordinated leg action are both results of correctly applied fundamentals and will not, in themselves, make the golf swing work. Consciously maneuvering the feet and legs should be reserved for totally experienced golfers who get added thrust and drive by making the legs work harder. The average golfer will develop a better, more natural swing by establishing positions which encourage natural movements.

15

Fundamental #10—Pushing the Clubhead into a "Toe-Up" Position

The result of the golf swing can usually be predicted within the first few inches of the backswing by the initial movement of the clubhead away from the ball. The movement indicates very quickly whether established positions will promote coordination unique to the golf swing and whether positions will have *time* to coordinate by the speed of the swing when it starts. The initial movement starts a swing pattern which determines accuracy at the top of the swing. An indication of accuracy *through* the swing is whether or not the clubhead starts away from the ball headed toward a "toe-up" position through the backswing. This position represents turning away from the ball with the clubface square.

Pushing into the toe-up position is a mechanical process for learning how to swing through it to obtain accuracy at the top of the swing, rhythm through the swing, and power at impact. The process is developed mechanically through three stages in this and the next two chapters: (1) by establishing accurate positions and pushing into the toe-up position; (2) by "breaking" the wrists; and (3) by pushing into a completion of the backswing. With practice, once the procedure is developed mechanically, positions and movements are easily smoothed together into a well-coordinated backswing.

How positions coordinate as the backswing starts makes established positions at address of critical importance to the overall swing. Although all positions are designed to coordinate with the backswing turning movement, the arms swing upward to establish positions at the top of the swing and accuracy at the top of the swing can only be obtained if the hands and arms are positioned accurately at address.

The position of the hands at address—which is more or less determined by fundamental procedure—helps establish accurate positions at the top of the swing by remaining unchanged as the left arm pushes the clubhead into the backswing. Although the left arm pushes the clubhead back, the position of the right arm (lower than the left) keeps the right elbow down to wedge the clubhead upward—and *both* arm positions contribute to the backswing movement.

How to Achieve Fundamental #10:

1. Use the waggle to reestablish positions. Roll the elbows toward each other with the right arm lower than the left, and firm the grip.
2. Use the forward press and, almost simultaneously, deliberately push the clubhead away from the ball with a firm, fully extended left arm. As the left arm pushes, let the weight that rocked forward rock back to the right—but prevent the left knee from "dip-

(1)   (2)   (3)

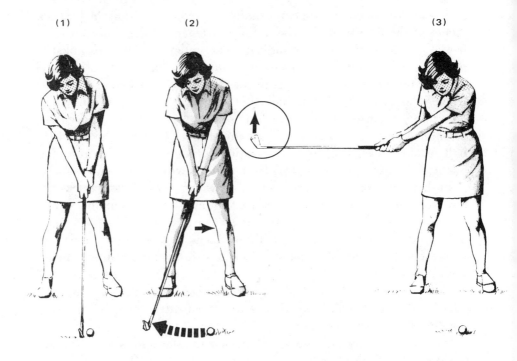

"ping" back with the turning shoulder movement by keeping the left knee forward.

3. Although the clubhead *starts* on the line of flight, it quickly swings up and onto the directional line with the shoulder turn as the right arm folds with the elbow down. Push the clubhead away until the shaft is parallel *to* the ground, *on* the directional line, *with the toe of the club pointing straight up.* The clubhead will be directly on line with the toes. The left arm, hands, and wrists remain unchanged through the movement. Consequently, if observed from above, the arm and shaft are straight as a result of the forward press.

Golfers unaccustomed to the somewhat unnatural movement of the backswing may suddenly sense a patting-the-head-while-rubbing-the-stomach feeling of coordination while keeping the left knee forward with the right elbow down. Keeping the left knee from swinging inward, however, is only a stage to go through in learning to swing the legs. After the backswing is completed and the procedure understood, practice quickly develops feeling for a coordinated, swinging movement.

Purposes:

A.   Keeps the clubface "square."

B. Promotes natural hand and wrist action.
C. Starts an accurate swing pattern with maximum swing arc.
D. Prevents a "flying" right elbow.
E. Puts the power and "swing" in golf by preventing the left knee from dipping.
F. Turns the shoulders.
G. Starts a natural pivot that leads to building body torque.
H. Initiates good tempo, timing and rhythm by preventing a fast backswing.
I. Introduces key swing thoughts.

A: Keeps the clubface "square": In order for the clubface to return "square" at impact, the square angle of the clubface established at address must be maintained through the backswing and established at the top of the swing. The clubface is "square" through the backswing when the clubhead is in the toe-up position and the shaft is parallel to the ground. From this position, the hands cock upward to establish the same clubface angle at the top of the swing. The clubface angle at the top of the swing will generally return to the same at impact, and *inaccuracy* at the top of the swing is represented by an open or closed clubface which causes slicing, hooking, pulling, or pushing the ball.

Since it is physically difficult to swing into and establish clubface positions at the *top* of the swing to see and check for accuracy, the toe-up position is a good checkpoint for open or closed positions. Accuracy through the toe-up position is a strong indication of accuracy at the top of the swing and golfers should frequently swing *into* the toe-up position to check for accuracy. If the toe points left with the clubface facing downward, the clubface is closed through the backswing and will be closed at the top of the swing. If the toe points right with the clubface facing skyward the clubface will be open. Accuracy through the toe-up position is essential for accuracy through the swing and is the easiest checkpoint in golf.

B: Promotes natural hand and wrist action: From the time the clubhead leaves the ball until it returns to the hitting zone, there should be no effort made to use the hands. Positioned accurately at address, the hands are then controlled by the movement of the left arm pushing the clubhead back. As the wrists "break" through the backswing, the hands move through and into accurate positions and they are pulled down from the top by the lower body moving back toward the ball.

Pushing the clubhead into the toe-up position keeps the left thumb on top, the same as at address, and positions the right hand accordingly. In this position the hands are placed the same as if they were drawn back independently in a hitting action (which employs the natural use of the hands through the swing). The clubhead quickly "fans" into the toe-up position, making an accurate swing pattern with the thumbs on top and the clubface "square."

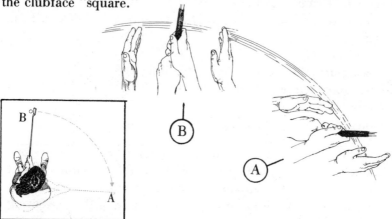

The toe-up position of the clubhead employs the natural use of the hands in a hitting action by drawing the hands back with the thumbs on top (A). This hitting position of the hands through the backswing is the same "thumbs up" position the hands establish at address and to which they return at impact (B).

The angle of the left arm and shaft and the "cocked downward" position of the left hand, which establish accurate hand positions, have been changed so often by various fundamentals that it may be helpful for a moment to review the processes used in arriving at accurate positions:

1. The left hand was initially cocked downward in order to position the club with an upright stance.

2 . When the clubhead was first positioned behind the ball, a straight arm-shaft position was established as seen from both the front and side.

3 . Flexing the knees in toward each other lowered the body into a "sitting down" position, moving the left arm naturally down and inward toward the body, thus establishing a *bent* angle of the arm and shaft as seen from both the front and side. Although the left wrist bent slightly downward, the hand retained a cocked downward position.

4 . Completing the grip and using the forward press resumed the
straight arm-shaft position as seen from the front, but not the
angle of the hand and shaft as seen from the side (which retained
the bent position).

Since the position of the left arm, wrist, and hand remain unchanged as the left arm pushes the clubhead back, the angle of the arm and shaft will be straight as seen from above and bent as seen from the front. Both positions promote good hand action and an accurate wrist break.

Front view.

Top view.

The arm and shaft angle halfway through the backswing.

C: Starts an accurate swing pattern with maximum swing arc: Pushing the clubhead away from the ball with a firm, fully extended left arm builds clubhead speed by obtaining a maximum swing arc, particularly when starting the clubhead on the ground and on the line of flight. An accurate swing pattern, however, moves the clubhead through the toe-up position. In order to attain the two objectives, it is helpful to know when the clubhead *should* swing off the ground and onto the directional line.

Sound golf instruction which teaches "taking the clubhead straight back on the line of flight," if taken too literally, can be the cause of many common errors—frequently keeping the clubhead *and* the golfer on the line of flight too long. Forcing the clubhead to stay on the line of flight beyond where it should swing up and inward blocks a natural shoulder turn, pulls the head off-line, and causes swaying across the right foot with a closed clubface. In order to prevent these things, regardless of ball position or club selection, a good rule of thumb is to let the clubhead leave the ground and line of flight with the shoulder turn, "fanning" toward the toe-up position (on the directional line) as the clubhead passes the right foot.

Playing woods and longer irons positions the ball forward in the stance and keeps the clubhead on the ground and line of flight longer than when using shorter irons which are positioned farther back. Learning to let the clubhead swing up and inward when swinging past the right foot, however, will keep the left arm extended and the clubhead low for a maximum swing arc with all golf clubs while turning into an accurate swing pattern with the clubface "square."

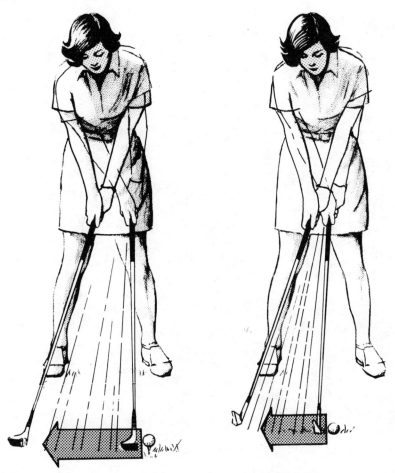

A maximum swing arc is obtained by keeping the clubhead on the ground and on the line of flight until swinging past the right foot. This keeps the longer-shafted clubs which are played farther forward (left), on the ground longer than the shorter-shafted clubs (right).

Golfers who have difficulty making a "big extension" through the backswing while at the same time preventing a lateral sway and pulling the head off-line will have less difficulty by learning to make a timely exit *off* the line of flight and onto the directional line. With accuracy in mind, it is helpful to remember that the directional line is the other half of the target line. The clubhead stays on the ground and on the line of flight only as far as the right foot. At that point the clubhead should leave the ground, swing off the line of flight into the toe-up position, and onto the directional line. This keeps the clubhead on the target line with the clubface "square" while extending the left arm into an accurate swing pattern.

D: Prevents a "flying" right elbow: Although the right arm folds as the

Origin of the "controlled groove."
Keeping the right elbow down wedges the clubhead upward into a controlled groove which can be repeated time after time to build a consistent swing.

backswing starts, the right elbow has a strong natural tendency to "fly" or "float" upward through the backswing rather than pointing down toward the ground. Keeping the right elbow down, however, welds the body and the arms together as a cohesive unit through the backswing to prevent their working independently—and is absolutely essential to a sound, repeating swing.

Power and momentum generated through the swing stem from different sources, but they must be delivered simultaneously at impact for maximum distance off the tee. The body supplies the power by winding up the muscles, but the clubhead builds momentum by combining natural arm and hand action with the body turn. A "flying" right elbow separates firm arm action from the body turn which, in effect, separates power from momentum.

A "flying" right elbow that lifts upward through the backswing separates power from momentum by separating the arms from the body turn.

A "flying" right elbow is indirectly caused by extending the right arm the same as the left at address, which inadvertently positions the elbow to be pushed outward and upward as the backswing starts, rather than pointing downward. It is difficult to keep the right elbow down unless the right arm is positioned lower than the left and the elbow pointing down to begin with; in that position, pushing the clubhead back with the left arm pushes the right elbow down.

A "flying" right elbow refers only to the elbow lifting upward through the backswing, not how far it moves outward and away from the side. The elbow must move away from the body to prevent restricting the swing. When the clubhead is in the toe-up position, the elbow points toward the ground still close to the body, but the extended left arm starts pushing the elbow away. Forcing the right elbow to stay tucked in tightly on through the backswing to prevent it from "flying" is a result of misunderstanding the term and restricts a full golf swing.

The position of the right elbow is a good place to look for trouble when shots are erratic for no apparent reason. When the right elbow flies upward, there is little control in the swing because the hands and arms swing free from the body to produce a loose, erratic swing. The result depends upon whatever may happen to coordinate rather than on firm control.

Although any poor shot may result from a "flying" right elbow, it commonly causes pulling with a closed clubface. When the right elbow is

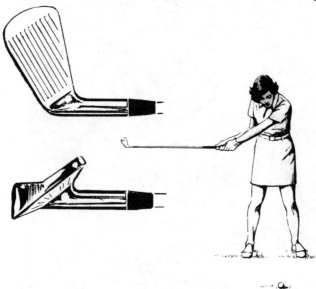

Keeping the right elbow down wedges the clubhead squarely through the backswing (top) but a "flying" right elbow keeps the clubface closed (bottom).

"flying" upward through the backswing, it is difficult to wedge the clubface "square" through the toe-up position. This keeps the clubface closed through the backswing, prevents a shoulder turn and pivot, and compounds the problem at impact by swaying back and forth. Swaying laterally back through the ball with a closed clubface "hoods" the clubface through the hitting zone, thus removing the loft of the club. This combination, particularly with a fast backswing, is generally the direct cause of a "smothered hook or pull" which seldom leaves the ground. Although pulling and "smothering" are common results, suddenly pointing the elbow down at the *top* of the swing loops the clubface open and pushes or slices instead.

The difference between a right and wrong position of the right elbow is frequently so slight as to be undetected by even experienced golfers, and it takes a very alert and knowledgeable golfer or instructor to spot this particular deficiency in an otherwise flawless swing. A "flying" right elbow should be suspected, however, when both arms extend at address. Positioning the arms correctly, however, with the right arm lower than the left, helps wedge the clubhead upward into a controlled groove which can be repeated time after time to build a consistent swing. *E: Puts the power and "swing" in golf by preventing the left knee from dipping:* A well-timed, rhythmical swing depends on relaxed and supple legs to promote good footwork and a swinging movement. Because of the word "swing" and the use of a "tool" in the hands, many golfers are mentally prone to allocate the swing to just the hands and arms, making the feet and legs inactive. Golf is such a mental game, however, that for golfers who may have difficulty in using the feet and legs, it is helpful to occasionally remind the subconscious that the swinging movement of the legs helps push and pull the arms and club and puts the "swing" into golf.

Key positions have been established to promote a swinging movement. The body is balanced in a "sitting down" position with the knees "unlocked" and the stance is upright with "feeling" in the feet as a result of accurate weight distribution. The forward press slides the knees toward the target, putting the legs in motion and starting a rhythmical movement. As the left arm pushes the clubhead back, the legs flow with the movement to continue a smooth and rhythmical "one-piece swing." Oddly enough, however, this naturally comfortable feeling of coordination, which stems from accurate positions, can prevent a powerful swing.

When positions are established that encourage a comfortable swinging movement, golfers are prone to just "go along" with the action. Because of the upright swing, however, and a comfortably coordinated feeling, there is a tendency to help the arms swing upward by dipping the left knee down and inward or jutting the left knee forward along with the backswing movement. Few things, however, affect the weight shift more adversely than dipping or jutting the left knee.

Letting the left knee dip down or forward at the beginning of the backswing shifts the weight to the left instead of to the right and instantly lowers the body. With the weight on the left when the downswing starts, the downswing action starts by pushing off the strong left foot, shoving the body away from the ball as the weight shifts right. This rather dramatic "firing and falling back" routine throws the clubhead upward from the top of the swing, down to the ground behind the ball, and causes "looking up" by pushing the head up as a result of the reverse weight shift.

Coupled with the dipping left knee and reverse weight shift, the body

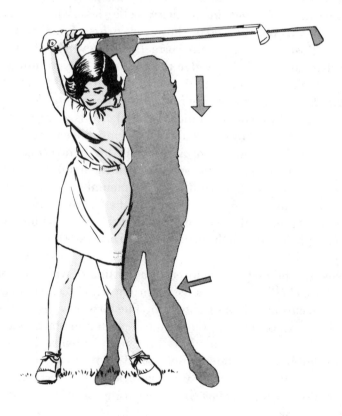

Keeping the left leg cocked toward the target as the weight shifts right prevents a reverse weight shift and swaying up and down by preventing the left knee from dipping down and inward.

lowers considerably as the weight shifts left. Pushing off the left foot then straightens the left leg on the downswing, throwing the clubhead over the top of the ball as the body pulls away from the ball and suddenly springs upward. Topping or hitting behind the ball results from dipping the knee just slightly. The more the left knee dips or juts, the more the body lowers and raises and the further the body is shoved up and away from the hitting zone. When this happens, "whiffing" the ball completely is a much more common result.

Anchoring the base of the body turn by briefly restricting left knee movement fortifies the left leg with strong driving power when the downswing starts. This essential driving power is lost, however, if the unrestrained left knee dips or juts with the backswing movement. Women, who generally possess a more willowy set of muscles than men, are prone to dip the left knee on the backswing, but this ladylike maneuver frequently spills over into the masculine side of golf to affect the swings of men as well.

In order to initiate strong leg action combined with a swinging movement, there must frequently be a conscious effort made in the learning process to keep the left leg cocked just slightly toward the target after the forward press and as the left arm pushes back. This prevents the knee from dipping down and jutting forward at the start of the swing in order to teach the feeling for an accurate swinging movement. The action of the left leg through the backswing will eventually be smoothed into a naturally coordinated movement as the leg swings inward. At this particular moment, however, keeping the left knee where it is teaches how to avoid an action that prevents a powerful swing.

F: Turns the shoulders: Pushing the clubhead into the toe-up position with a firm, fully extended left arm turns the shoulders and starts a natural pivot. Completing the shoulder turn and pivot is then a matter of pushing the clubhead on through the toe-up position to a completion of the swing. Although golfers should neither expect nor be expected to swing outside their physical capability, all golfers attain their own potential by completing the shoulder turn. Forcing the shoulders to turn beyond what is natural or comfortable, however, not only ruins a good golf swing but generally frustrates the young golfer and immobilizes the old.

The length of the backswing depends on overall accuracy and does not necessarily indicate whether the shoulder turn is completed or not. Golfers who establish accurate positions, however, and push through the toe-up position with a firm left arm will generally complete the shoulder turn. As the left arm pushes the clubhead back, the tucked-in right elbow wedges the clubhead upward and the simultaneous action of *both* arms in the swing contribute to the action.

The importance of pushing with the left arm to turn the shoulders can quickly be determined by first swinging the club back with the right arm, which does not turn the shoulders, then pushing the club back with the left arm which turns the shoulders naturally.

Pivoting
Pushing the clubhead away from the ball with a firm left arm promotes a natural shoulder turn and pivot.

Swaying
Taking the clubhead back with the predominantly stronger right arm prevents a shoulder turn and pivot and promotes a lateral sway.

Pulling the club back with the hands, or initiating the backswing with the predominantly stronger right arm prevents a shoulder turn and, with the weight shifting right, promotes a lateral sway. Swaying is the opposite of pivoting, or turning, and results in a sliding movement of the body on the target line. Unless the shoulders turn by pushing the clubhead back, the body starts a lateral movement from the moment the clubhead leaves the ball.

Maintaining an upright stance with the angle of the right foot closed and the right knee flexed inward prevents a lateral movement as the weight shifts to the right when the shoulders start turning the moment the backswing starts.

G: Starts a natural pivot that leads to building body torque: Square positions at address enable the hips to turn as far right as left from the center of their rotational ability, thereby starting a natural pivot by encouraging the hips to turn rather than slide as the backswing starts. Because of the easy coordination between the shoulders and the hips, many golfers mistakenly believe that further promoting this coordination with a big, full pivot along with the shoulder turn results in a big, powerful golf swing. But such is not the case. Letting the shoulders turn the hips, by preventing a quick pivot, is a key to building power.

Through the backswing, muscular tension develops between the shoulders and the hips by winding up the long back muscles. These muscles unwind with tremendous power on the downswing, accelerating the clubhead through the ball with maximum clubhead speed as the arms and hands are pulled down and through the hitting zone. Letting the hips turn *with* the shoulders as the backswing starts, or freeing the hips to turn too far by dipping or jutting the left knee down or forward prevents this muscular windup.

Pushing the clubhead into the toe-up position starts a slight pivot, but delaying a full hip turn by keeping the left knee forward until the wrists are breaking enables the pivot to coordinate with momentum created by the wrist break which augments a muscular windup. Although the hips and shoulders turn together in a "one piece swing," timing influences coordination and if the hips should turn too quickly before the shoulders turn them, they will have passed beyond the point where this muscular coordination takes place naturally to build additional power.

Tensing muscles through the backswing is a power source in golf. The term "muscle tension," however, may be somewhat of a misnomer for more thinking golfers who might develop more power by considering the term "body torque." The difference between tension and torsion, as it relates to golf, means the difference between just swinging on back through the hitting zone or uncorking tremendous stored-up power through the ball by building body torque for stronger lower body action.

The dictionary defines tension as "stretching." Torsion, however, is defined as "the tendency of a twisted object to straighten out." This natural tendency of torqued or twisted muscles to spring back where they came from not only adds more power by compounding normal tension, but the momentum of the clubhead swinging back "holds" the shoulder position at the top of the swing that fraction of a second necessary for the torquing action to start the hips back first as the initial downswing movement. If the hips turn *with* the shoulders or initiate the backswing, the shoulders and the hips complete the turn together. With nothing at the base of the turning movement for the shoulders to turn

The pivot

Keeping the left knee forward as the backswing starts builds body torque, producing tremendous clubhead speed as the hips make a one-quarter turn through the backswing and a three-quarter turn back through the ball.

against, tension will develop as the muscles stretch—but not the body torque that produces lower body action by twisting upper body muscles.

While learning to develop body torque, it is important to understand that keeping the left knee forward is a very slight action used only to restrain the hips from turning too soon, before the shoulders turn them naturally, and to prevent the hips from turning too far along with the shoulder turn. Anchoring the base of the body turn just as the backswing starts is the key to this backswing movement. The left leg does swing inward and additional fundamentals develop the movement naturally through the wrist break.

Relatively speaking, compared with how far the hips turn back through the ball, they turn very little through the backswing to add additional power. Square hips at address, which enable the hips to turn as far right as left from the center of their rotational ability, produce more power when restricted by making a one-quarter turn on the backswing and a three-quarter turn back through the ball.

H: Initiates good tempo, timing and rhythm by preventing a fast backswing: The speed of the swing is regulated and "set" the moment the backswing starts. With accurate positions established, coordination is promoted by timing—not speed or strength—by deliberately pushing the clubhead away with a slow movement away from the ball. A fast backswing is the "bane of the game" and will usually prevent the very things a golfer is striving for, such as consistency, accuracy, and power, by not giving positions time to coordinate. The old hustler's slogan, "Give me a man with a fast backswing and a fat wallet!" is not to be taken lightly. Many an experienced hustler has based his wagers and his tactics on the speed of the opponent's practice swings while waiting to tee off!

Although power is gained by building body torque, neither speed nor strength is needed to wind up muscles or swing the golf club. For example, golfers who are physically capable of breaking a club in half with their bare hands are apt to feel that physical strength alone gains distance off the tee. But by combining a fast backswing with unqualified brute strength they defeat the very purpose they hope to gain—and breaking a club in two becomes sheer pleasure as they frustratingly succumb to an inability to even hit the ball, or find it if they do!

The clubhead must never be "muscled" through the backswing with such speed that positions do not have time to coordinate, for timing is the essence of coordination. It is difficult to obtain objectives with precise movements when the clubhead is actively engaged in yanking positions out of alignment. Combining good mechanics with a deliberately smooth beginning will synchronize positions which promote power and accuracy by allowing time to negotiate the otherwise complex movements of the swing—particularly such things as keeping the left knee forward at the start of the swing, to anchor the base of the body turn.

The word "swing" is an interesting term in golf which can elicit two different physical responses to starting the clubhead back. A swinging movement can start with either a pushing *or* pulling action, just as starting a child's swing. Given a choice, golfers may prefer to pull the clubhead with the hands, inadvertently creating a fast backswing by whipping the clubhead back. Pushing, however, prevents the whipping action but still starts a swinging movement. Thinking of pushing as very deliberate and almost in slow motion, just as pushing a child's swing, helps immeasurably in starting a smooth and well-timed swing.

I: Introduces "key swing thoughts": Up to this point, building the swing has presented only a foundation for the swing itself and conscious thought has been needed to establish accurate positions. Now that the swing is underway, however, fundamentals already applied must be trusted to do their jobs in order to free the mind to concentrate on other things. It should be remembered that concentration is an asset in golf which should be reserved for things that cannot be relegated to fundamentals.

Trusting established positions enable golfers to develop what are called "key swing thoughts," which is deliberate concentration applied to anything specific that either helps the golf swing work when actually playing golf or helps develop the swing in practice.

Until the swing is sound and positions are correct, key swing thoughts should be used in practice as accurate check points and guidelines for developing a well-grooved swing. At this stage of the swing there are four swing thoughts which can be used to "check and groove" the backswing: (1) As soon as the clubhead leaves the ball, check to see that the left knee is not dipping down or jutting forward; (2) check to see that the right elbow points toward the ground; (3) check to make certain the toe of the club points upward; and (4) start a deliberately slow backswing. Conscious thought in *practice* applied to positions or movements eliminates conscious thought when *playing* by building confidence in doing things instinctively. When playing golf, concentration can be directed toward a key swing plan directed toward results.

When playing golf, key swing thoughts are invaluable in limiting thinking by programming a good swing plan, but golfers have to find the keys that "trigger" their own golf swing. It is generally agreed that using more than one swing thought, or changing thoughts while swinging, will only complicate a natural swing. Although some key position or movement through the swing may be the thought that makes the golf swing swork, a golfer should never lose sight of the fact that the purpose

Mis-hitting the ball occasionally, which is encountered even by experts, should always be recognized and accepted as being only humanly less than perfect.

of golf is to *swing* the club and *hit* the ball—and avoid getting lost in a maze of thoughtful, mechanical confusion by making specific positions or movements work. The highest level of proficiency occurs when the least amount of thought is given to the mechanics of the swing.

Trouble in the swing is seldom encountered in the same way all the time because fundamentals are seldom coordinated in the same way all the time. Many factors are involved that affect and change the swing and when trouble does occur, part of the unique challenge of golf is to find and correct the problem by adjusting positions or using different movements which correct a faulty swing. Such is the value of being able to be analytical. The golf swing, however, should *never* be analyzed or corrected as a result of only an occasional poor shot. Mis-hitting the ball occasionally, which is encountered even by experts, should always be recognized and accepted as a direct result of being only humanly less than perfect. In order to avoid unnecessary mental entanglements, key swing thoughts—just as fundamentals—should be used in practice to develop a swing which may be trusted when actually playing golf.

16

Fundamental #11—The Wrist Break through the Backswing

Instructional golf is generally reluctant to classify the wrist break as a fundamental, preferring instead to leave the movement to just "a natural end result of good hand action." Although the reason is valid in that hand and wrist action are combined and natural, it does not necessarily follow that the wrists will break with accuracy—and an *accurate* wrist break is frequently overlooked as an underlying factor in "good hand action."

Understanding the wrist break is not for the purpose of learning how to break the wrists or use the hands, but to continue understanding the overall swing. Although natural, the wrist break is a connecting movement between the body and the hands and it is important to know how the wrists break accurately as well as naturally, where the wrists should break, and how positions affect the movement. Because the wrist break is natural, its importance as a connecting movement is usually obscured by the fact that the action lies within the larger connecting movement of the backswing as a whole—which usually commands more attention by connecting positions at address with positions at the top of the swing.

Studying the wrist break as an independent movement "stops the camera," so to speak, making the backswing less complex by seeing how and where the wrists should break for "good hand action" in an accurate backswing.

How to Achieve Fundamental #11:

Waggle positions into place, making certain the grip is correct. Use the forward press to straighten the left arm-shaft position and push into the toe-up position. Keep the straight arm and shaft on the directional line and *move only the hands to* cock the clubhead upward. The clubhead will not move far, but how far is unimportant as long as the hands are fully cocked upward, the left wrist is straight, and the hands are on the directional line.

The wrist break

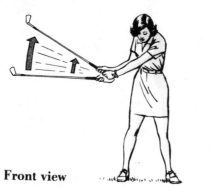

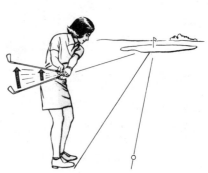

Front view

Side view

Purposes:

A. Relates "good hand action" and an accurate wrist break to positions at address.

B. Determines how the hands cock into an accurate swing pattern.

C. Develops power by coordinating wrist break with shoulder turn and pivot.

D. Determines role of wrist break in starting or stopping swing action.

A: Relates "good hand action" and an accurate wrist break to positions at address: No effective golf swing can be developed without good hand action, a part of which is an accurate wrist break. Neither action, however, can be manipulated or forced to contribute effectiveness because both actions are and must be natural. The hands are pushed into and through fundamental positions by other swing movements and all fundamentals, particularly those which affect the shoulder turn and pivot, affect hand action. The hands will cock through an accurate wrist break, however, only when they are positioned accurately at address, whereupon an accurate wrist break will be a natural result of "good hand action."

Power in golf is generated by the body and transferred to the clubhead through the hands so that an accurate wrist break is needed for "good hand action" to deliver the power at impact. As well as being a combined natural movement, the hands and wrists are also independent factors in attaining accuracy and delivering power as determined by positions at address. A faulty grip is frequently the cause of an inability to negotiate an accurate golf swing because the hands are not in position to let the wrists break accurately through the natural movement. It might be helpful to review Chapter 3 on "Analyzing the Grip," which stresses the responsibility assuming the grip has to the golf swing as a whole.

Aside from establishing the grip at address, the position of the hands is a determining factor in how and where the wrists break by presetting the angle of the wrists. The cocked up and down angle determines *where* the wrists will break and is influenced by how far the golfer is "sitting down to the ball," whether the body is leaning over or standing upright, and how far the arms extend to position the clubhead. The straight line of the left arm and shaft, either established initially or reestablished by the forward press, determines *how* the wrists will break. Building the swing with fundamentals assures the hands are well positioned before they are pushed into and through the backswing, where a naturally accurate wrist break will promote accuracy through the backswing.

B: Determines how the hands cock into an accurate swing pattern: The swing pattern is the path the clubhead follows through the backswing, downswing, and follow-through, which is determined by positions and movements. Movements through the backswing establish a single position at the top of the swing with a sequential movement of the arms turning the shoulders, which turn the hips. The movements reverse on the downswing as the lower body starts back first, pulling the arms, hands, and clubhead down from the top of the swing which is followed by the shoulder turn. An accurate wrist break will keep the left wrist straight and promote an accurate swing pattern by keeping positions at address, through the backswing, and at the top of the swing correctly interrelated. This will enable the muscular winding and unwinding process to return the clubhead accurately.

Fundamentals in the basic golf swing create a swing pattern which move the hands upright toward the right shoulder, laying the shaft of the club over the right shoulder and parallel to the ground and the target

"Laying off" at the top of the swing in a flat swing pattern.

line. From this position the arms and hands are more easily pulled back down to return the clubface square. Because the wrists break naturally, the left hand grip and preset wrist and hand positions along with the shoulder turn determine the swing pattern by determining the angle at which the hands cock upward, through the toe-up position of the clubhead, between a flat and upright swing.

Since the left hand establishes the foundation for the grip and is the dominant factor in the action of the hands, the left hand grip can be used to simulate the position of both hands on the club to demonstrate how the position of the hands and wrists affects the swing pattern.

The straight arm-shaft position at address, either established by the waggle or reestablished by the forward press, straightens the left wrist in line with the arm and shaft. Maintaining this straight line through the wrist break by letting the hands hinge upward on the directional line keeps the left wrist straight and moves the clubhead up and back into an accurate swing pattern.

Although breaking the wrists mechanically from the toe-up clubhead position moves the hands straight upward on the directional line, when actually swinging through the backswing the shoulders and hips are turning as the clubhead is pushed *through* the backswing to the top of the swing. The rotational movement of the body, turning *away* from the ball, diverts the path of the clubhead back behind the directional line as well as upward into the right swing pattern.

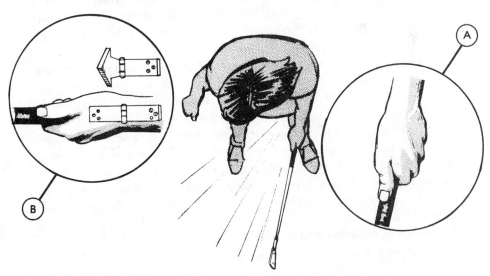

A straight arm-shaft position as the clubhead leaves the ball (A) keeps the left wrist straight, hinging the clubhead upward into an accurate swing pattern (B).

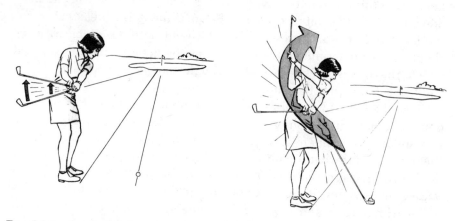

Breaking the wrists mechanically from the toe-up position moves the clubhead straight upward on the directional line. Pushing *through* the toe-up position, however, diverts the clubhead into the right swing pattern as the body turns away from the ball.

Although the basic swing pattern is very precise, there is no standard plane or pattern regarding "flat," "upright," or length of the backswing which can be determined absolute for each individual. The angle and length of the swing pattern also depend on physical build and capability. Frequently there is undue concern over flat or upright swings, or underswinging or overswinging, as good or bad for all golfers. Golfers develop their own golf swing, but the clubhead should never go far afield from what is physically accurate for each individual's swing by connecting positions with an accurate wrist break.

C: Develops power by coordinating wrist break with shoulder turn and pivot: Although the hands cock upward through the backswing from the point where the wrists break naturally, instructional golf frequently leaves the wrist break to a somewhat elusive place just "somewhere through the backswing" by not teaching how and where the wrists *should* break. Not quite certain where this action should take place, golfers have a tendency to allow the wrists to break too soon, or occasionally too late, to promote good timing and coordination. Although the wrists break naturally, power builds up through the backswing by timing the wrist break with the shoulder turn and pivot by learning to let the hands cock upward from the point where the shaft of the club is parallel to the ground.

The wrist break naturally corresponds with the way each individual establishes the position of address, and a determining factor in where the wrists *do* break is the preset up and down angle of the wrists at address which position the hands to cock early or late through the backswing.

This preset angle of the wrists is determined by how much the golfer is leaning over or standing upright, the extension of the arms, and how much the knees are bent. Although the golf swing should always be based on fundamentals to establish accurate positions, not all golfers establish the same setup as defined for the basic swing. Physical build and comfort are also factors at address which affect the position of the hands and determine their action through the swing. In order for the hands to cock upward through the backswing, they must be cocked downward at address. But regardless of how positions are established, the hands should neither be cocked too far downward or too far upward as a result of poor positions.

Leaning over too far or positioning the hands too close precock the hands to a degree where they are almost fully cocked upward at address (A). With the hands already cocked upward, the parallel shaft position is established very low and early, the result of which is an early shoulder turn, less wrist action, and generally a shorter, more compact swing (B). Conversely, cocking the hands completely downward by standing too upright or raising the wrists too high (C) establishes a parallel shaft position further into the swing (D). This delays the shoulder turn and pivot, the wrists break later in the swing, and the result is more of a fluid swing, more with the arms.

Individual setups which deviate from basic positions may not necessarily be inaccurate or even incorrect. However, they do cause an early or late wrist break either below or above the hips, as opposed to the

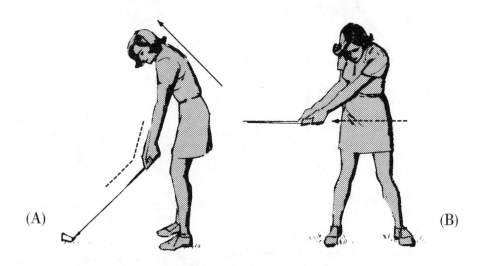

(A)

(B)

Setting a low angle of the hands by leaning over too far (left) promotes an early wrist break below hip level (right).

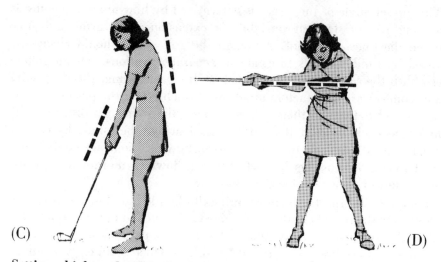

(C)   (D)

Setting a high angle of the hands by standing too upright (left) promotes a late wrist break above hip level (right).

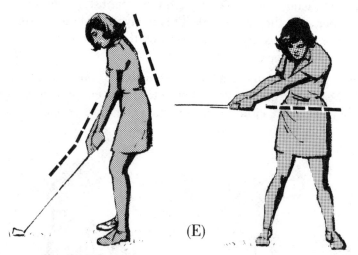

(E)

Although an early or late wrist break may not be incorrect, fundamentals which *prevent* leaning over or standing too upright promote a wrist break from hip level.

basic position in which the hands and parallel shaft are more in line with the hips . (E)

In general, golfers should try to avoid establishing extreme positions which preset the angle of the wrists too high or low (cocking the hands very early or late) as further indication that positions themselves are accurate. Exactly where each golfer attains the parallel shaft position, however, is really incidental to a good golf swing as long as positions are not extreme and the hands can still cock upward from the point where the left arm is fully extended and the shaft of the club is parallel to the ground. Pushing the clubhead into the toe-up position with a firm left arm starts a natural shoulder turn. Learning to let the wrists break from the parallel shaft position promotes coordination that helps keep the left arm firm by timing the hands cocking upward with the shoulder turn and pivot. Promoting a wrist break either before or after the shaft is parallel prevents coordination that keeps the left arm firm by increasing momentum that "breaks" the left elbow and causes overswinging.

The angle of the wrists in the basic golf swing encourage the wrists to break very gradually from the start of the swing, which, in effect, they do. Because of this, however, they are also encouraged to break very quickly, especially with a fast backswing. Allowing the hands to cock upward before reaching the parallel shaft position results in "picking up the club" at the beginning of the swing, narrowing the swing arc and decreasing clubhead speed but increasing momentum that "breaks" the left elbow at the top of the swing with additional stress. Although "picking up the clubhead" is a more common cause of "breaking" the left elbow, a very *late* wrist break toward the top of the backswing makes it just as difficult to keep the left arm firm.

Few golfers are able to incorporate a very quick or very late wrist break into the backswing without "throwing" the clubhead from the top and "falling away from the ball." Rather than releasing the clubhead through the ball the hands release too early, either "uncocking" the clubhead into the ground behind the ball or catching the top of the ball on the upswing as the weight shifts right instead of shifting left.

Knowing when the hands should cock upward prevents any mental leeway which allows the wrists to break too soon or too late, and keeps the action of the hands concentrated through the parallel shaft and toe-up clubhead position. Experienced golfers who appear to deviate from basic positions or movements, such as those who appear to use a quick wrist break and "set the angle early," are still applying fundamentals. Some golfers, for instance, have adapted fundamentals to intentionally establish the parallel shaft position very low and early to create strong body action. As long as the left arm is extended, the shaft parallel to the ground, and the wrists hinge upward from this early "set," an accurate swing pattern and full swing radius can still be maintained. In deviating from fundamentals, however, most golfers are simply courting trouble by establishing poor positions. Adhering strictly to fundamentals will attain the best results and most golfers could improve their swing considerably by heeding an old Scottish adage: "Leave yerrr axe at home, Laddie, and brrring yerrr brrroom."

When the wrists hinge upward from the parallel shaft position the

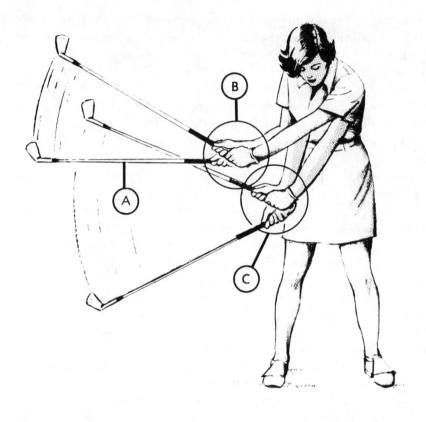

Extending the left arm into a parallel shaft position (A) before the hands cock upward (B) prevents "picking up the club" and narrowing the swing arc by breaking the wrists too soon (C).

blocked position of the closed right foot and the extended left arm turn the shoulders, which turns the hips, and the hands cock upward with the shoulder turn. As the clubhead is pushed on through the backswing, a timely wrist break coordinating with the body turn winds up the muscles on the backswing, adding power to the swing.

D: Determines role of wrist break in starting or stopping swing action: The wrist break through the backswing is part of a continuous, swinging movement. It is also part of the foundation of the swing, in that hand, wrist, and clubhead action can be "felt out" during the waggle in a little "bottom of the swing" maneuver behind the ball by breaking the wrists back and forth while setting up to the ball. Just as the forward press gets a "running start" on swing movement by putting the legs in motion, the waggle gets a "running start" on swing accuracy with hand and clubhead action at address.

During the waggle, the clubhead is continually pushed back low toward the directional line and turned and aimed toward the toe-up position with the left wrist straight, breaking the wrists just slightly and returning the clubface square. This movement of the hands, without the shoulder turn, "programs" the hands and clubhead to move into and through an accurate swing pattern.

Waggling and the wrist break provide a final opportunity to get "set" for an accurate golf shot. The "sense and feel" procedure of waggling trains the mind and muscles to start the swing automatically. With practice, on one of the waggle movements the swing will start of its own accord. At this point, positions must be flawlessly established and movements coordinated because beyond the wrist break, through the

Waggling the clubhead back and forth with hand and clubhead action (left) gets a "running start" on the backswing until the backswing starts of its own accord with a firm left arm and shoulder turn (right).

backswing, momentum combines with the body turn to increase tempo, making it virtually impossible to stop the swing for "overs" to correct a faulty beginning.

"Stubbing" the clubhead going back makes it particularly hard to stop the swing to start again because the clubhead stops momentarily, pulling the hands behind the ball. As the club snaps away from being stuck on the ground, the additional force of breaking loose sends the clubhead quickly through the wrist break into a reflexive movement. Since stubbing the clubhead is generally caused by firmly "planting" the clubhead on the ground, particularly with tufted grass behind the clubhead, or by positioning the hands behind the ball, using an up-and-down or back-and-forth waggle helps prevent "stubbing" problems. And a deliberately slow move away from the ball makes it possible to stop the swing to start again by minimizing the force of the backswing action.

17

Fundamental #12—Completing the Backswing

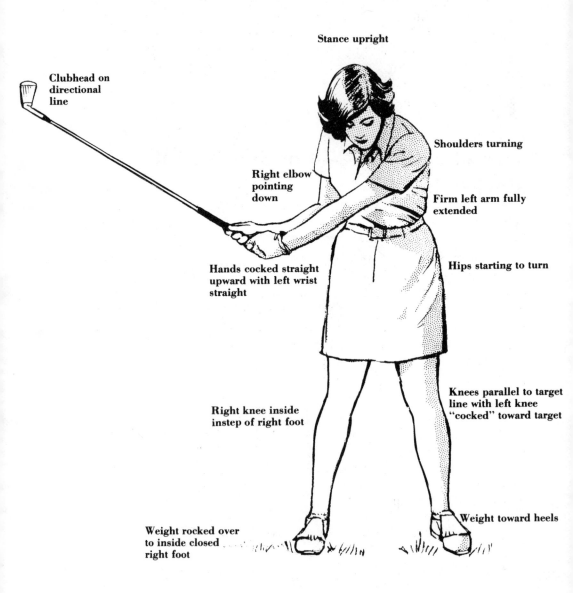

Stance upright

Clubhead on
directional
line

Shoulders turning

Right elbow
pointing
down

Firm left arm fully
extended

Hands cocked straight
upward with left wrist
straight

Hips starting to turn

Right knee inside
instep of right foot

Knees parallel to target
line with left knee
"cocked" toward target

Weight rocked over
to inside closed
right foot

Weight toward heels

Fundamentals establish the above position from which point the left arm
pushes the clubhead into accuracy at the top of the swing.

Completing the backswing is a continuation of pushing the clubhead through the toe-up position with a firm left arm. Consequently, when applying the new fundamental that completes the movement, emphasis must be placed not only on its application, but on the accuracy of pre-established positions.

Positions established at address and through the wrist break have, in effect, "built" one whole position. If this preestablished position is accurate, the fundamental movement that completes the shoulder turn will complete the backswing, automatically establishing accurate positions at the top of the swing that complete the swing with power and finesse.

How to Achieve Fundamental #12:

Rebuild the swing up to this point by waggling positions into place. Use the forward press and push the clubhead into the toe-up position, being particularly careful to prevent the left knee from dipping down or inward or jutting forward. Break the wrists mechanically, and make certain that all positions defined on the opposite page are accurately established. From this position, push the clubhead upward with the firm left arm to complete the shoulder turn. Let the shoulders turn the hips, and let the left leg swing inward. Keep the left knee aimed ahead, however, to lift the left heel inward and off the ground. The clubhead will swing behind the directional line with the completed shoulder turn.

Purposes:

A. Establishes correct positions at the top of the backswing.
B. Swings the left leg inward with the left heel off the ground.
C. Builds body torque.

A: Establishes correct positions at the top of the swing: Pushing the clubhead on through to the top of the swing with a firm, fully extended left arm automatically establishes the following positions by completing the shoulder turn:

1. Grip firmly in fingers with left thumb under shaft

Straight left wrist

6. Shaft of club parallel to ground and to line of flight

7. Straight left wrist maintains "square" clubface

8. Right palm under shaft with thumb offset

2. Left arm firm but may "flex" somewhat

9. Head remains steady

3. Right elbow points toward ground but moves away from the side

10. Completed shoulder turn with back toward target

11. Hips turned by shoulder turn

4. Right knee inside right instep

12. Left leg swings inward with left knee aimed ahead

5. Weight "rocked" to right but contained inside right foot

13. Left heel lifts off the ground

The exact position at the top of the swing which returns the clubhead squarely and powerfully through the ball is so dependent on so many things that less than perfect golfers are seldom able to assume this exact position with a consistent degree of accuracy. Although the average golfer should not expect to play perfect golf by always attaining this top of the swing perfection, every dedicated golfer should *strive* for near perfection to compensate for things that do go wrong. Consistency, not perfection, is a more realistic goal for average golfers. The more fundamentals that combine with a firm left arm and full shoulder turn, the more likely golfers are to reach their own level of proficiency by consistently swinging as close as possible to an accurate top-of-the-swing position.

The golf swing is demanding, but not to the point where it has no flexibility. Although the accompanying illustration depicts a perfect position at the top of the swing, it also portrays the perfect golfer. Individual golfers need not attain these exact results to still play creditable and enjoyable golf. Studying each position at the completion of the backswing will help each golfer see where the golf swing can be flexible to negotiate his own golf swing.

(1) *Grip is firmly in the fingers with left thumb directly under the shaft:* This position has no flexibility. The three fingers of the left hand, in particular, must be very firm to prevent "dropping the club" or "letting go at the top." The position of the left thumb reinforces this firm grip and the two together prevent overswinging or dropping the club below the parallel line. The "spring" effect of the left thumb holds the position at the top of the swing during the transition of the backswing to the downswing—and it is a good position to learn to "feel" at the top.

(2) *Left arm firm but may "flex" somewhat:* This position can have flexibility, and the old adage about "keeping the left arm stiff" is inaccurate in describing how the left arm should react. The action of the left arm is really a matter of semantics: it must be straight as opposed to bent, it can be flexed as opposed to rigid, and the summation of the two is that it must be firm. How much flex develops in the left arm depends on the position of the elbow at address, individual strength to withstand momentum, and timing and tempo (which determines how much stress develops). A deliberately smooth backswing, however, and a full shoulder turn helps keep the left arm firm at the top of the swing by pushing the clubhead to the top with the shoulder turn rather than flinging it up with the arms.

(3) *Right elbow points toward ground but moves away from the side*: How far away from the side the right elbow moves is determined by the length of the shot which determines the length of the backswing. Short shots to the green, for instance, with a short backswing, keeps the elbow in close but a full shot with a maximum swing arc moves the right elbow away from the side to prevent restricting the backswing by restricting the shoulder turn. There is a vast difference, however, between the elbow pointing *down* and moving outward or moving

outward from the body by "flying" or lifting *upward*. For a well-controlled swing, the right elbow must point down toward the ground at address and through the backswing to position the elbow at the top to drive downward on the downswing.

(4) *Right knee stays inside right instep*: There is no leeway for this position. Once the knee goes beyond the right instep the weight is rolling across the right foot and pulling the body to the right. A good checkpoint in practice is to check the relationship of the knee to the instep to make certain the body is not swaying off the ball through the backswing.

(5) *Weight "rocked" to right but contained inside right foot:* It would be boringly repetitive to review the many reasons why this position and movement cannot be flexible. The weight must shift to the right in order to shift back to the left, and a slight "rocking" movement is sufficient to start the weight transference. A slightly closed right foot with the knee flexed *inward* at address allows the weight to transfer to the right but prevents the weight from rolling across the right foot through the backswing.

(6) *Shaft of club is parallel to the ground and to the line of flight:* Although the backswing is shorter when using shorter irons, swinging the shaft of woods and longer irons parallel to the ground and to the line of flight at the top of the swing generally indicates accuracy at address and through the backswing. Besides promoting accuracy, swinging parallel makes it easier to shift the weight from the top by positioning the hands to pull downward. Since it is not easy to see positions at the top of the swing, however, golfers are more apt to be concerned with getting the club to the top rather than where it is when it arrives. Consequently, the angle of the shaft is a good position to have checked occasionally to detect discrepancies in the swing.

Although all golf swings are certainly individualistic, generally speaking, swinging either short of or below a parallel line indicates either a restricted swing or overswinging, and swinging either in front of or behind a parallel line indicates an incorrect swing pattern. Although many golfers swing "off parallel" and still return to a good position, it takes almost perfect timing and control to swing too far from parallel and still coordinate good lower body action with good hand action to pull the hands and clubhead accurately through the ball.

Any position or movement which determines the swing pattern affects swinging parallel to both the ground and line of flight. Physical build and capability, as well as individual "style," are also determining factors. Young, flexible golfers or those with somewhat "fluid" swings frequently swing below parallel and senior golfers with less muscular flexibility should not expect to extend the swing so far. Very strong golfers with fairly compact swings frequently swing very short of parallel with excellent results. Although physical build and capability have some bearing on swinging parallel (and swinging short of or beyond is not all bad if not too excessive) an angled alignment of the shaft to the ground or to the line of flight is usually caused by swing defects. Most golfers who fail to reach or swing beyond parallel are just losing power by not applying fundamentals.

Swinging "short of parallel" results from such things as swaying, an incomplete or restricted shoulder turn, too wide a stance, swinging flatfooted, or an incorrect wrist break which flattens the swing pattern. Overswinging—or "swinging below parallel"—is caused by letting go with the left hand, a very quick or very late wrist break that bends the left elbow, swinging too fast, collapsing the left wrist, or overturning the

Swinging short of parallel.

Overswinging or swinging below parallel.

shoulders or the hips by dipping the left knee or angling the right foot open.

Overswinging is much more common and by far a more serious problem than a shorter, restricted swing because the hands swing too far beyond a point where lower body action moving back to the left can pull the hands downward. When the hands swing too far beyond the top of the swing it is difficult to shift the weight back to the left because the hands pull upward as the downswing starts, throwing the clubhead upward and outward from the top of the swing. When that occurs the momentum from the clubhead action prevents the weight from shifting left by keeping it on the right.

Overswinging is seldom the result of just one thing, making it difficult to correct at times. If not too excessive, however, overswinging is usually corrected by positioning the left thumb neither too "long" nor too "short" for good control at the top (see Fundamental #1D in chapter 4); firming the left arm and grip at address; a slow move away from the ball; an accurate wrist break; and correcting positions and movements that promote a shoulder turn while preventing excessive overturning of either the shoulders or the hips.

If overswinging remains a problem regardless of corrections, practicing a three-quarter swing helps develop a shorter swing to position the hands correctly. It simply takes more practice to correct overswinging without the use of the fundamentals.

Swinging the shaft of the club parallel to the line of flight denotes an accurate, well-controlled backswing. Starting the swing with a straight left wrist and cocking the hands straight upward through the toe-up position combines with a full shoulder turn and accurate arm and elbow action to lay the club back along the right shoulder and parallel to the line of flight.

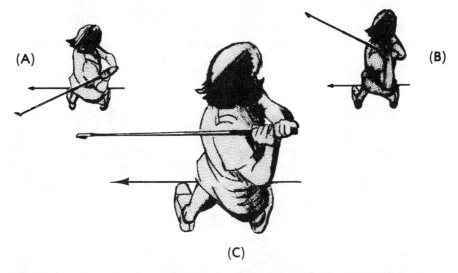

(A) (B)

(C)

A flat or restricted swing swings the club behind a line parallel to the line of flight (A). Overswinging swings the club beyond a line parallel to the line of flight (B). A straight left wrist through an accurate wrist break, however, helps position the shaft parallel to the line of flight at the top of the swing (C).

(7) *Straight left wrist maintains "square" clubface:* The clubface angle at the top of the swing corresponds with the clubface angle at address and through the backswing—and a "square" clubface at the top of the swing is more apt to return square at impact. See Fundamental #10A in chapter 15.) An "open" clubface at the top refers to the toe of the clubhead pointing straight toward the ground (A); a "closed" clubface

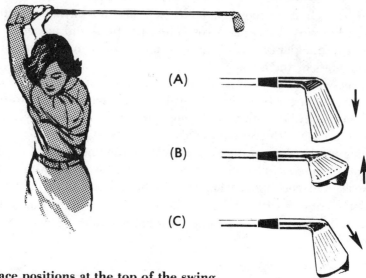

Clubface positions at the top of the swing.
An open clubface at the top of the swing points the toe toward the ground
(A), a closed clubface aims the face toward the sky (B), and a square
clubface is halfway in between (C).

turns the clubface toward the sky (B); and halfway in between the two is
the accurate "square" position (C).

Although inaccuracy at the top of the swing causes inaccurate shots,
golfers should not become unduly concerned with open or closed
clubface positions at the top of the swing because they are not the cause
of inaccuracy at impact. Incorrect clubface positions at the top of the
swing are incorrect positions themselves and it makes little difference
whether the clubface is open *or* closed at the top of the swing if it is
anything *other* than accurate.

Just as incorrect positions anywhere in the swing must be prevented or
corrected to attain accuracy at impact, the same is true with the
clubface, and knowing what *prevents* inaccuracy is the essential
importance of understanding clubface positions. In order to prevent
inaccuracy at the top of the swing, a firm, straight left wrist must be
established at address and maintained through the backswing. The
clubface angle, along with the line of the shaft, is a good position to have
checked occasionally to determine accuracy through the backswing.

A firm left arm and full shoulder turn pushes the shaft of the club up
to the top of the swing, parallel to but behind the directional line where a
"square" left wrist becomes the key to a square clubface. A firm,
straight left wrist—straightened at address and maintained through the

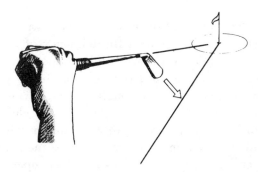

Maintaining a straight left wrist to the top of the swing keeps the clubface square, aiming the toe of the club toward the directional line.

wrist break—"squares" the clubface at the top and points the toe of the club toward the directional line with the clubface "looking" slightly skyward. A straight left wrist at the top of the swing will return the clubface squarely and powerfully through the ball with the wrist still straight, the arm and shaft in line at impact, and the hand in the strongest backhand hitting position.

Keeping the left wrist entirely straight at the top of the swing is a difficult position to maintain. As the body turns away from the ball and the clubhead continues upward, a slight concave "kink" may develop in the left wrist as it gives through the backswing to compensate for the two opposing directions. Although it is more comfortable to let the wrist kink inward—and the average golfer should not be overly concerned if unable to retain the stronger position—a bent left wrist at the top of the swing "opens" the clubface slightly, pointing the toe of the clubhead toward the ground. A good swing pattern can still be maintained, but the more the left wrist kinks at the top of the swing the more difficult it becomes to square the clubface at impact.

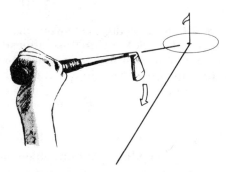

"Kinking" the left wrist slightly at the top of the swing opens the clubface slightly with the toe of the club pointing toward the ground.

The position to be avoided at the top of the backswing is a *completely* open or closed clubface. Along with the tendency of the left wrist to kink, there is also a tendency toward total collapse unless the wrist is straight as the hands cock upward through the toe-up position of the clubhead. When the hands cock through the backswing with the left wrist bent inward (often as a result of gripping the club with the left hand too far right), the hands swing upward incorrectly with the left palm under the shaft where momentum increases the bend. Either the swing will "flatten" as the wrist collapses which opens the clubface completely (although it may appear to be closed with the flattened swing pattern), or if an upright swing can be maintained the same open clubface is established at the top. Either position at the top of the swing returns the clubface open to slice the ball because the clubface is too far out of alignment to square the face at impact. Slicing also occurs with the left wrist straight if the swing pattern is flat because the clubface generally cuts across the ball at impact. An otherwise perfect downswing with the weight shifting left and the arms pulling downward will often accentuate collapsing the wrist which commonly causes "toeing" the ball off to the right.

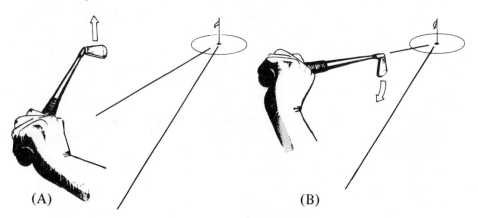

(A)   (B)

Collapsing the left wrist through the backswing may flatten the swing pattern, swinging the hands back low with the clubhead behind the target line. Although the angle of the clubface may appear to be closed (A), the clubface is open at the top of the swing just as it is with an upright swing and the same wrist action (B).

(8) *Right palm under shaft with thumb offset:* In addition to left hand and wrist accuracy, a corresponding position which strongly reinforces the hands at the top of the swing is sometimes referred to as a "waiter's tray position" of the right hand, describing the position of the right hand under the shaft as if, when open, the hand were holding a tray. The

position is a good checkpoint, not only indicating strong, accurate hand positions, but also indicating a completed shoulder turn with the right elbow pointing down. Along with the right hand position, positions and movements which enable the right palm to swing under the shaft by being accurate themselves, such as an accurate grip and full shoulder turn, will often correct a chronic slice.

The offset right thumb prevents the right hand from stopping the swing too soon, enabling the shaft to reach a position parallel to the ground for a full backswing.

A "waiter's tray position" of the right hand is a good checkpoint, not only indicating accurate hand positions but also a full shoulder turn with the right elbow pointing down.

(9) *Head remains steady:* Maintaining a steady head position is a key pivotal position throughout the swing which keeps the arc of the swing intact by swinging the shoulders around and under a somewhat fixed position. Although keeping the head steady may be a good swing thought occasionally, this deliberate action, in itself, seldom compensates for incorrectly applied fundamentals. A steady head is only an indication that the body is not swaying *off* the ball on the backswing, moving *over* the ball through the hitting zone, or moving up and down through the swing. A steady head is more apt to occur as a result of establishing positions that prevent a swaying movement, whereupon,

keeping the head down by "keeping an eye on the ball" becomes a useful swing thought.

A simple check for head movement is to face away from the sun and align the top of the head shadow to a point on the ground while practice-swinging. If the head shadow moves off that point, positions must be corrected to prevent the back-and-forth or up-and-down movement.

Shadow test for moving head.

(10) *Shoulder turn completed with back toward target:* A full shoulder turn will normally turn the back toward the target as the shoulders turn a full ninety degrees from the address position. Although all golfers may not be this muscularly adept, even senior golfers must complete the shoulder turn within their physical capability to establish accurate positions for their own golf swing. An incomplete shoulder turn prevents lower body action from starting back first, which starts the right

shoulder forward from the top of the swing and much too soon. Slicing may result from throwing the clubhead from the top but pulling is more likely as a result of the shoulder action.

(11) *Hips turned by shoulder turn:* A full pivot on the backswing is the natural result of a full shoulder turn because the shoulders turn the hips.

B: *Swings the left leg inward with the left heel off the ground:* Understanding the final two positions in the illustration of the completed backswing will help immeasurably in developing natural leg and footwork.

(12) *Left leg swings inward with left knee aimed ahead:* While completing a study of the movement of the left leg through the backswing, it should be remembered that learning the use of fundamentals is for the purpose of understanding golf swing movements, not to encourage conscious action such as either restricting or promoting the movement of the legs. Preventing the left knee from dipping by restricting left knee action and preventing a quick hip turn by keeping the left knee aimed ahead are movements unique to the golf swing in order to·build body torque. Once the action is understood, however, every effort should be made to practice and "groove" the action into a natural swinging movement. Swinging legs and the shoulder turn and pivot are not independent actions.

The left knee, in particular, continues to be the key to good leg action. The seemingly complicated movement of "cocking" the left leg toward the target and aiming the left knee forward is far less complicated if thought of as only a fleeting second at the very beginning of the swing; the left leg *must* swing inward to put the "swing" in golf.

The small movement away from the ball is the most critical moment in the swing because it directly influences timing—and timing affects coordination. A deliberately slow move away from the ball, if only for the first few inches, allows time to coordinate essential positions and movements the *moment* the backswing starts. It takes *time* to cock the left leg toward the target with the forward press, contain the weight inside the right foot as the weight rocks to the right, keep the left knee where it is, then keep the left knee aimed ahead as the left leg swings inward with the hip and shoulder turn. Good leg and footwork, then, more than compensate for lack of speed and muscle going back by preventing such things as overswinging or a reverse weight shift while adding driving power to the legs, building body torque, and keeping the arc of the swing intact.

The coordinated movement of the knees, legs, and feet in golf takes work and practice to "groove" good leg and footwork. Trying to maintain or establish positions with conscious thought while swinging rather than grooving them into subconscious, reflexive movements, exaggerates actions and changes rhythm through the swing. In this case, it keeps the left knee anchored too long in the swing, keeps the left heel on the ground, and prevents the leg from swinging inward. Pushing the clubhead into a completion of the swing pulls the left leg into a swinging movement as the shoulders turn the hips. *Aiming* the left knee forward, as opposed to *keeping* the knee forward, will not prevent the swinging movement. Experimentation and practice, along with checking and waggling positions, soon promotes a natural use of both the feet and legs. (13) *Left heel lifts off the ground and inward:* Good leg action lifts the left heel slightly off the ground and inward as the leg swings inward. The action of the left knee, however, determines the action of the heel by determining the movement of the leg. Keeping the left knee forward to the top of the swing may either keep the left heel on the ground and prevent the leg from swinging or keep the weight on the left and lift the heel too high. Although the left heel should lift off the ground, consciously lifting the heel juts the left knee too far forward, preventing the leg from swinging inward.

Many variations in form and swing technique occur among golfers who either keep the left heel on the ground or lift the heel too high. Better swings develop, however, by learning the natural action of the left heel lifting inward with a swinging leg movement. As the weight shifts to the right, balance is maintained and a "ready" position established for the downswing as pressure builds against the inside ball of the left foot. *C: Builds body torque:* The answer to the question of whether the golf swing is natural or unnatural does not necessarily lie in an individual's inherent ability. Certainly some have more natural coordinative ability but in golf, particularly, coordination develops by applying fundamentals which coordinate positions and movements. Nowhere is this more pronounced than at the exact junction of the swing where the arms swing upward as the body turns away from the ball. With very few exceptions, the arms are rarely called upon to swing upright together as the body turns rotationally. Outside of golf, natural movements of the body seldom require this same coordination.

Many positions and movements are directed toward the arms swinging upright in golf, but the natural muscular reaction of the hips to the arms is to let the hips turn freely with the action of the arms. Although a natural movement, particularly noticeable in the "classic" swing era of Harry Vardon, a "modern power swing" has developed which restricts hip movement to add more power by building body torque.

It should be acknowedged, before further discussion, that developing a modern, powerful golf swing is not necessarily a compelling goal of golfers—even dedicated golfers—nor should it have to be. Many find it comfortable to let the hips turn freely and others should promote more of a turning movement. Whether building power or not, however, preventing the left knee from dipping as the backswing starts *is* of fundamental importance (see Fundamental #10E in Chapter 15), and this action in itself creates a certain amount of torque. A full shoulder turn combined with aiming the left knee forward as the leg swings inward builds additional torque, and many golfers find that building additional torque by keeping the left knee *too* far forward is a difficult, unnecesssary complication in the swinging movement. Just as golfers have a choice in using the forward press, golfers also have a choice in determining for themselves how much restrictive left leg action is comfortable or beneficial in their own golf swing.

Additional body toque, described under Fundamental #10G in Chapter 15, cannot be attained if the hips turn freely and completely with the shoulder turn—but very little restraint is needed to put the coiling mechanism to work. Keeping the left knee forward until the arms swing upward will prevent the hips from turning too soon as well as preventing the left knee from dipping down or jutting forward. Keeping the left knee aimed ahead as the leg swings inward will prevent the hips from turning too far with the shoulder turn. The action restricts the hips just long enough for a full shoulder turn to completely wind up the muscles between the shoulders and the hips.

A prominent difference in the golf swings of men and women is in the natural use of the legs. Women generally develop a less powerful, more fluid swinging movement, whereas a man's natural physical strength develops an inclination toward using the legs more forcefully. In between the two is the forceful, swinging movement which both should develop in practice. A natural, powerful swing develops, regardless of physical ability, by establishing positions which promote a natural pivot, then restricting this natural movement with restricted left leg action at the beginning of the swing. This times the pivot with arm movement to develop body toque.

THE BACKSWING PUSH-AWAY

The forward press.

Pushing the clubhead into a "toe-up" position.

The wrist break through the backswing

Completing the backswing.

18

Practicing the Backswing

Now that tools are available to work with, building a sound golf swing is a matter of learning to use these tools with proficiency. The swing is neither built nor repaired by keeping the tools inside the toolbox. They must be taken out and used.

Golfers who have been using the book for reference rather than as a textbook may have missed the importance of the step-by-step procedure in building the basic swing, searching instead for things they think affect their own golf swing. Should this be true, it would be well to review Chapter 2 on "How Fundamentals Build A Sound Golf Swing" because misapplication of even one fundamental may adversely affect the whole golf swing. It is not enough to presume that positions thought to be correct are, in effect, contributing to a sound golf swing. The chapter emphasizes this salient point.

The success of the downswing and follow-through is largely determined by a correct backswing through a "cause and effect" reaction. Once the downswing starts, a good result reflects accurate positions and a good backswing. Although it may be difficult to refrain from hitting balls or playing golf, feeling the completed swing is improved, practicing just the setup and backswing at this stage of the game pays good dividends later on.

Individual golfers, by now, may have found at least one or several fundamentals which have been improperly applied in either the grip, position of address, or backswing. These incorrect positions have been so ingrained in the swing that, like comfortable old shoes, they may be difficult to part with or replace. New fundamentals, however—just like new shoes—soon become comfortable with use.

The application of just one new fundamental which is foreign to the swing will make the entire swing feel different, but golfers must have confidence in using new positions. Confidence develops by becoming familiar with how a new position feels at the exact place where it is incorporated into the swing, by deliberately establishing the position by itself then gradually adapting it to its immediate surrounding area.

Units of the backswing which have been introduced and can be practiced separately are: the grip, position of address, waggle, forward press, toe-up position of the clubhead, wrist break, and the top-of-the-swing position. Each of these sections encompass a group of fundamentals or use a fundamental movement. Starting with the grip, each unit which uses a new fundamental should be practiced repeatedly until that part of the swing is comfortably correct. Only then should that unit and those which precede it be connected with the next. Connecting units in the swing should be a slow and gradual process, very deliberate and precise, to develop feeling for how corrected fundamentals fit and affect the others. When all of the units are known to be accurate and can be deliberately connected, a sound setup and reliable backswing is simply a matter of smoothing out the process into a continuous, well-timed action.

Lengthy chapters have been devoted to describing single movements and positions in order to understand and, when necessary, correct fundamentals. Because of the necessary emphasis on "bits and pieces" of the swing, it is not unlikely that one or two fundamentals may have gained importance over others in the minds of different golfers. The golf swing, however, is a combination of many things and no fundamental, no matter how seemingly important to individual golfers, should be given precedence over others as the solution to a sound golf swing. No matter how exciting it may be by now to have discovered a "secret" to the swing, this exciting new solution must not gain importance over other fundamentals in order to develop a rhythmical swinging movement. The only workable secret in golf is the rhythmical application of *all* of the fundamentals.

Rhythm is not to be confused with tempo in the swing. Tempo is the speed with which different golfers swing naturally, and varies between fast and slow. Rhythm, however, is the smooth acceleration of the clubhead within the tempo of the swing that builds up power and speed with good coordination to create good timing. When the swing is sound, practicing the backswing to combine rhythm with tempo is just as important as establishing and practicing good positions because the remainder of the swing is almost totally dependent upon a rhythmical backswing.

Although tempo may vary considerably between individual golfers, or even in an individual's swing from time to time, rhythm cannot vary within the tempo of the swing. Maintaining rhythm, however, within the natural speed of the swing also depends on developing and protecting one of the more elusive, vulnerable parts of the swing—concentration—which is not easily obtained and hard to regain if lost.

Rhythm, tempo, and concentration are initially determined by an individual's natural temperament and disposition, and reflected in the pace and rhythm of walking as well as swinging the club. The fragile nature of concentration is such, however, that it is easily shattered by any of many factors which affect tempo and rhythm. Sudden "outside" distractions or irritations, changes in the weather, even the pace and disposition of other golfers on the course may quickly affect concentration and change tempo and rhythm. This, too, can be detected in how a golfer changes pace in walking as well as swinging the club, either of which may quickly be affected by a current frame of mind. Taking such things into consideration, tempo and rhythm in the swing are determined not only by natural, physical tendencies but by a change in attitude. It is important to remain consciously alert to the fact that tempo is affected by a sudden change in concentration which results in and is reflected by a sudden change of rhythm in the swing itself.

Developing concentration is a talent in itself, but golfers who have developed the talent are frequently regarded as being rather "stuffy" by appearing unfriendly. Staying away from distractions such as idle conversation, however, is one of the easier ways to maintain both rhythm and concentration (and friendships can be restored on the nineteenth hole by resuming conversation and picking up the tab).

Reestablishing rhythm and timing when concentration has been disturbed can sometimes be accomplished just by changing the pace of walking and restoring rhythm in the waggle; by smoothing the rhythm of walking down the fairway, walking up to the ball and using the same rhythm in the waggle when setting up to the ball. Concentrating on the rhythmical movements of walking and waggling by moving slower to slow down a fast backswing or moving faster to be a little more aggressive, times rhythm with tempo and improves the swinging movement.

Playing golf should not have to be a frustrating, club-throwing event, but many golfers make it so by not preparing themselves to meet the personal challenge of the game through practice. Frequent practice not only develops confidence and a rhythmical, well-timed swing by using fundamentals and practicing rhythm and timing, but practice

Frequent practice develops confidence and a rhythmical, well-timed swing.

strengthens the hands, coordinates positions, "grooves" the swing, and develops "muscle memory" by practicing instinctive fundamental movements. More than that, however, the more a golfer practices *off* the course, the more reliable his swing will be on the course. When a golfer arrives on the first tee with a sound golf swing and full of confidence, the less concentration is needed for setting up to the ball and swinging and the more concentration can be applied to enjoying the game at hand. Practice makes the difference.

Part 4
The Short Swing

19

The Purpose of the Short Swing

When the arms remain extended through the full golf swing, the hands make close to a full circle from the top of the backswing to a completion of the follow-through. The short swing is practiced in the bottom half to three-quarters of this circle where the hands swing below shoulder level, swinging through the wrist break on both the backswing and the follow-through.

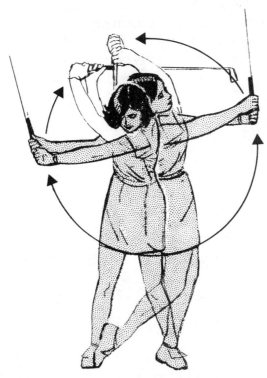

The hands complete a circle in the full golf swing but the short swing is practiced below shoulder level to develop coordination, timing, and rhythm.

The short swing introduces two new fundamentals—the toe-up position of the clubhead in the follow-through and hitting with the right hand—while explaining the start of the downswing. Swinging through this short section of the swing applies every fundamental position and movement with the exception of positions at the top of the swing, thereby producing a miniature or "short" complete golf swing.

Although the downswing and follow-through are generally only reflections of accuracy preceding the action, starting the downswing without guidelines to follow is like starting across country without having studied a road map. It is simply easier to negotiate the full golf swing by knowing where the swing is going before the downswing starts.

Practicing and developing the short swing gives purpose and direction to the swing down from the top while building a final unit that can readily be extended into a full golf swing. It is a good training aid because it eliminates the tendency to put power in the swing while focusing attention on the importance of coordination, timing, and rhythm as keynotes in the swing and developing power by practicing good hand action and accurate swing movements.

Part 4 teaches how to practice and apply fundamentals in the short swing as a preliminary means to negotiating the full golf swing. Since this section of the swing uses most of the fundamentals, it is an excellent practice area as well as a good place to check for accuracy.

20

Fundamental #13—The "Toe-Up" Position of the Clubhead in the Follow-Through

The toe-up position of the clubhead in the follow-through corresponds with and is opposite the toe-up position in the backswing. Establishing and studying the toe-up position as a fundamental position helps the golfer understand how the clubhead continues through an accurate swing pattern while learning how to swing through the position as a natural result of applying other fundamentals.

How to Achieve Fundamental #13:

Establish the toe-up position of the clubhead in the backswing as shown in Chapter 15. From that position, keep the elbows together, swing the legs to the left, and let the swinging movement pull the arms and clubhead into an opposite "toe-up" position in the follow-through. Keep the head from moving and shift the weight to the left. As the weight shifts left, bring the right knee through the ball along with the clubhead and let the hips turn through the ball by turning the right knee toward the target. A full extension of the left arm passes naturally to the right arm so the right arm is fully extended in the toe-up position. Just as in the backswing, the toe-up position is on the directional line.

The toe-up position of the clubhead in the follow-through corresponds with and is opposite the toe-up position in the backswing.

Purposes:

A. Promotes accuracy through the ball by pulling the hands and club-head toward the target on the target line.

B. Develops a feeling for starting the downswing with lower body action.

C. Helps shift the weight from inside the right foot to the left side.

D. Helps to establish and to maintain a steady head position.

A: Promotes accuracy through the ball by pulling the hands and clubhead squarely toward the target on the target line: Left arm extension passes naturally to the right arm just past the hitting zone as a tucked in right elbow and swinging legs combine to straighten and extend the right arm. Since the directional line is part of the target line, swinging into the toe-up position *on* the directional line helps hit out toward the target by keeping the hands and clubhead on the target line. Right arm extension, however, is a natural result of delayed hand action and centrifugal force uncocking the wrists through the hitting zone; it is neither the source of power nor accuracy when swinging through the ball.

Power and distance are obtained at the moment of impact with the left arm firm in line with the shaft, the hands ahead of the ball, and the left wrist straight. Accuracy is a result of shifting the weight to the left and turning the hips through the ball to pull this strong left side "position" powerfully through the ball squarely toward the target. A turning movement through the ball pulls the square left wrist from the top of the swing squarely around toward the target and prevents breaking down the wrist by "cupping" the right hand underneath the left as the right arm extends.

Turning the right knee toward the target with the clubhead swinging through and keeping the head from moving forward helps "hit against a strong left side" by letting the hips turn. However, the turning movement may still make accuracy difficult as the shoulders are prone to turn with the hips from the top of the swing.

A "diving" right shoulder moving forward from the top precludes the ability to hit out toward the target because the clubhead is thrown forward from the top of the swing, beyond the line of flight, and pulled back across the directional line. Turning the hips, however, while keeping the right shoulder "back and coming down," can be practiced by placing the clubhead in the backswing position and swinging into the follow-through position just as described in developing the fundamental action. As proficiency develops, the action should be extended through the wrist break in the short swing with the same proficiency.

B: Develops a feeling for starting the downswing with lower body action: The downswing starts with a movement of the lower body shifting the weight back to the left. Starting the downswing with lower body action, however, is not exactly the same because the downswing starts by reflex action rather than by conscious thought. Although a reflexive forward movement, the hips move diagonally from the top of the swing and turn through the ball. The movement is far less complex, however, when developed as a reflex action in a swinging leg movement.

Understanding how the hips react to the movement of the legs when swinging into the toe-up position develops confidence in learning to let the legs swing naturally between the toe-up positions in order to accelerate the clubhead through the ball with an accurate hip turn. The following experiment helps understand the movement:

(1) Establish the "sitting down to the ball" position of address. Using only the lower body, try swinging the legs without the use of the feet or hips. This futile effort quickly determines leg movement to be combined with the *action* of the feet or hips. (2) From the same sitting down position, but without swinging the legs, simply push to the left against the right instep. Then resume the position and move only the hips to the left. In each instance, the hips initiate the forward movement but also slide laterally rather than starting a diagonal, rotational movement back toward the target.

Conscious movement of the feet or hips not only starts a lateral rather than turning movement, but exaggerating the action of pushing against the right foot or moving the hips to the left dramatically accentuates the quick coordination of foot, hip, and leg action in lower body action. Since these actions are known to produce quick results, golfers are often encouraged to consciously use the feet or hips to make the downswing work. Such conscious thought or action, however, particularly from the top of the swing where movements are reflexive, quickly *over*emphasizes lower body action and changes rhythm through the swing by forcing the lower body to react *too* quickly to coordinate with other swing movements. Yet the combined action of the feet, legs, and hips *creates* the action needed to shift the weight back to the left, pull the arms down from the top, and turn the hips through the ball by swinging the legs toward the target. The problem then becomes one of how to start an accurate downswing with the lower body while avoiding the harmful side effects. The answer lies in learning how to let the legs swing naturally to obtain the same results:

(3) Using the same foregoing experiment, start letting the legs swing with the double action of pushing against the right foot and moving the hips to the left. With practice, the combined action soon transfers to leg action, with the heels lifting slightly, by using the feet and hips. Consequently, leg and foot action become the primary factors in moving the lower body forward. The swinging movement of the legs, using lower body muscles, prevents swinging with the arms and accelerates the

clubhead through the hitting zone by pulling the arms down from the top and turning the hips through the ball.

Turning through the ball is an essential movement in golf that prevents swaying laterally with a restricted hip turn. Hitting into the toe-up position prevents "spinning out" or "whirling" back through the ball and pulling the clubhead across the directional line by turning too far, too soon. Spinning back through the ball without swinging on the target lines commonly causes pulling, hooking, *or* slicing (depending upon the clubface angle) by pulling the clubhead inward across the target lines.

The swinging movement of the legs is natural and almost identical to throwing a baseball underhand down the target line from the position established at address. The weight shifts right as the right arm draws back to throw and the right knee turns back toward the target as the legs swing forward, pulling the right arm back by moving the hips back first and turning them toward the target. The slightest amount of effort obtains the best results.

The golf swing uses the same movements used when throwing underhand down the line of flight from the position established at address; swinging the legs and starting the hips back toward the target before the arm swings forward.

C: Helps shift the weight from inside the right foot to the left side: Fundamentals continually direct movements toward an accurate and natural golf swing, and many fundamentals have been introduced to promote a weight shift to the left. Regardless of fundamentals, however, shifting the weight is further promoted by extending the right arm through the hitting zone and hitting toward the toe-up position in the follow-through.

Allowing the weight to remain on a "stuck" right side is a real swing-wrecker because it forces the hands and arms, rather than the legs, to initiate the downswing. Swinging the legs and encouraging an extension of the right arm into the toe-up position, however, encourages a weight shift to the left and prevents "hitting from the top," "coming over the top," or "falling away from the ball."

Golfers who have difficulty timing the weight shift left with delayed hand action will find it helpful to study and practice the timing of the baseball swing. Placing the feet together and laying the golf club back in a baseball batting position, then drawing the golf club back to hit while stepping into the ball quickly stresses the feeling for what causes the "pause" at the top of the swing as the hands are pulled back through the hitting zone by the weight shifting left.

D: Helps establish and maintain a steady head position. Fundamentals position the head behind the ball at address where the shoulders turn around the head and under the chin throughout the golf swing. Since excessive head movement affects the swing adversely; golfers are generally told to "keep the head down" and "keep an eye on the ball" to prevent such problems as swaying or "looking up."

Keeping the head steady should be practiced by keeping the head "down" while swinging into the toe-up position: but keeping the head down too *far* may cause additional problems in golf by positioning the *chin* too low. This restricts the shoulder turn as the shoulders turn *into* the chin, both swinging back and swinging through. Either the body "sways" laterally or the head is pushed or lifted up, or the swing is "blocked out" as a result of the shoulder action. Lifting the chin a bit, however, when the chin is too low, will generally correct such problems.

Along with lifting the chin while setting up to the ball, experienced golfers may also "keep" the *left* eye on the ball and cock the chin to the right for a more comfortable head position. Because of the many factors that make up the golf swing there is no single position deemed best for everyone. Although fundamentals position the head fairly comfortably, experimentation and practice is helpful, within the short swing, to find the best position to keep the head steady while swinging back and swinging through.

21

Fundamental #14—Hitting with the Right Hand

Golfers occasionally become so involved in the mechanics of the swing that actually hitting the ball becomes only an ineffectual "net result" rather than a powerful addition to the swing. When the grip is correct, however, and the swing sound, the act of hitting is frequently the most singularly active thing a golfer can do to trigger a straight and accurate shot.

Hitting with the right hand is apt to portray a picture of the right hand "taking over" the golf swing, overpowering the left, and directing the ball far left of the target line. Rather than misdirecting the ball, however, hitting the ball is simply a right-handed action (for right-handed golfers) that is a necessary part of the action of the swing. At the same time, a hitting action through the swing assures the natural action of both hands through the hitting zone.

Instructional golf is so explicit in teaching golfers not to control the club with the hands that even experienced golfers with sound golf swings may be reluctant to use the right hand as they should to develop a hitting action. There is a vast difference, however, in using the hands to control the club by initiating the backswing or the downswing, and creating a hitting action by setting out to hit the ball.

How to Achieve Fundamental #14:

Follow the same procedure for swinging between the toe-up positions, as in Fundamentals #13, but set out to hit the ball with the right hand as the backswing starts.

Purposes:

A. Establishes essential hitting position within the swinging movement.
B. Establishes hitting position without a fast backswing.
C. Combines the natural use of both hands through the hitting zone to square the clubface at impact.
D. Helps "stay behind" and "swing through" the ball with good hand action.
E. Stresses importance of accurate grip.

A: Establishes essential hitting position within the swinging movement: Although the golf swing is a continuous swinging movement from the start of the swing, no effective swing can be obtained without starting a hitting action to establish a hitting position within the swinging movement. Hitting with the right hand is not for the purpose of hitting the ball better by hitting harder at impact, but for the more important purpose of cocking the right elbow down at the top of the swing to establish a hitting position of the hands and arms.

Understanding fundamentals helps eliminate conscious thought by knowing that certain positions which are not classified as fundamentals are naturally assumed by fundamental actions, such as the cocked-down position of the right elbow at the top of the swing—and setting out to hit the ball, with the right hand, is the action that cocks the elbow down. Although the right elbow is positioned at address to point downward through the backswing, cocking the elbow down at the top of the swing is not accomplished by merely preventing the elbow from "flying." Setting out to hit the ball creates an entirely different action than simply swinging the clubhead back with the elbow down.

In a hitting action, as opposed to a swinging movement, when the right hand draws back to hit, the elbow rather than the hand and arm starts the movement back to the left and positions the hand to hit at the top of the swing. For example, swing the right arm to the right and swing it back to the left. The arm and hand swing back and forth without the elbow bending. Now draw the right hand back to hit. As the arm and hand start back to the left, the elbow cocks down at the top of the swing and cocks the right hand into a hitting position.

Swinging the right arm back and forth keeps the right arm straight (left) but drawing the right arm back to hit cocks the elbow down at the top of the swing to establish a hitting position within the swinging movement (right).

The movement of the right arm on the backswing in golf is a combination sidearm underhand throwing and hitting action which, more simply defined, is a natural whipping movement caused by a hitting action. Overhand or sidearm throwing sports such as baseball, basketball, tennis, fly-casting, etc., all employ a natural hitting action in that when the right arm pulls back to either throw *or* hit it reaches a blocked position of the elbow and shoulder. This blocked position not only cocks the elbow down but also helps drive the hips forward and shift the weight to the left with the forceful elbow movement. The elbow and the hips then pull and whip the right arm down and through the ball. Underhand swinging movements, however, such as pitching softball, pennies, or horseshoes, keeps the elbow straight. In golf, the action of the right arm, although appearing to be an underhand swinging movement, is the same as any sidearm throwing or hitting sport where a throwing action cocks the elbow down at the top of the backswing. And in order to produce this natural action, there must be a deliberate effort made as the backswing starts to hit the ball at impact.

An excellent exercise to develop feeling for hitting with the right hand and keeping the elbow down, along with starting the downswing with the hips and shifting the weight to the left, is to establish the address position and practice throwing golf balls underhand with a throwing, hitting action. Swing the legs, and use the hitting action of the hand to throw the balls both long distances and short. Accuracy in throwing is not important. In fact, the exercise can be practiced without throwing balls, but the act of throwing in this manner quickly develops feeling for keeping the right elbow down and hitting through the ball with rhythmical body movements.

Throwing underhand develops good right side action by using a hitting action to keep the right elbow down.

B: Establishes hitting position without a fast backswing: Difficulty is always encountered by golfers who misinterpret a hitting action and set out to "kill" the ball with a fast backswing and additional force at impact. Such murderous determination, however, prevents rhythm and coordination, rushes the shot at the top of the swing, and kills the shot instead.

Speed and force are neither recommended nor necessary in either establishing a hitting position or gaining additional power. The demonstration described on the preceding page which compared swinging and hitting can be negotiated even in slow motion, clearly indicating a hitting position at the top of the swing to be a mental response to starting a hitting action. A very slow movement still cocks the elbow down, establishing the hitting position while maintaining rhythm and developing more power with better coordination.

An important thought to remember in golf is that a hitting action is more readily obtained by curbing the killer instinct and simply pushing the clubhead away from the ball with a firm left arm, slow beginning, and an intent to hit the ball. In this regard, when playing golf a basic physical and mental difference between men and women is the more aggressive "killer instinct" of men to use a hitting action as compared with the natural tendency of women to use a more gentle swinging movement. In teaching golf, this frequently requires helping women become more aggressive, stronger "hitters" and helping men become less aggressive, rhythmical "swingers."

C: Combines the natural use of both hands through the hitting zone to square the clubface at impact: Using natural hand action through the hitting zone is a matter of understanding how the hands work naturally outside the swing and then applying this action when hitting the ball.

In a natural hitting action, when hitting squarely through a given target with either the back of the left hand or the palm of the right hand, the hand naturally assumes the exact opposite position in the follow-through from any position of the hand as it draws back to slap or hit. Consider the action of the right hand, for instance; from overhead the hand moves squarely downward and from shoulder level the hand moves squarely across to the opposite side. Toward hip level, however, and especially below hip level where the hands are hitting in golf, the movement of either hand in a natural hitting action draws the hand back with the thumb on top, squares the hand at impact, and rolls the hand over with the thumb on top again. In order to hit accurately in golf, the right hand must impart this same "rolling over" movement used in a natural hitting action, rolling the right hand over the left rather than "scooping" over the top of the ball by "cupping" the right hand underneath. An incorrect grip results in incorrect shots by not positioning the right hand accurately for this natural hitting action.

As the lower body turns, pulling the hands down from the top, the hands are inactive and in a cocked position until they reach hip level. This intentionally delays the hitting action until the hands return to the hitting zone in a strong hitting position. The left hand has more or less completed its hitting responsibility simply by being pulled into a "straight-armed batting" position as a result of lower body action shifting the weight and turning. The right hand, however, has yet to

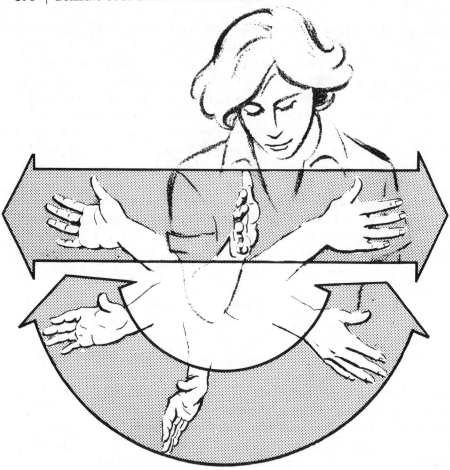

The right hand hits into the follow-through from the same position from which the hand draws back to hit. For instance, the hand hits straight back and forth from shoulder level but below hip level (where the hands are hitting in golf) a natural hitting action rolls the right hand over.

complete its natural action and must hit actively through the ball to complete the natural rolling-over movement.

When the mind is conditioned to the fact that the golf swing is a swinging movement combined with a hitting action, the arms and hands push into the backswing closely coordinated and together in the "one-piece swing." As the hands approach the hitting zone, however, with the wrists still cocked, the back of the left hand, palm of the right hand, and the clubface still aim forward. The action of the hands combine to square the clubface only when the right hand hits the ball. Pulling and hitting with the left hand and leaving the right hand *out* of the hitting action causes slicing or pushing by leaving the clubface open at impact. In fact, an otherwise perfect golf shot with no right hand action often resembles a bonafide shank by hitting on the *toe* of the club straight to the right. And, of course, for fear of "shanking" again, the problem of "toeing" is compounded as golfers swing a little faster with reluctance to hit the ball at all.

Although accuracy through the swing is essential to hitting accurately with the hands—particularly actions which shift the weight back to the left and pull the hands down from the top—an important fact to remember, and one that dispels a continuing concept in golf, is that hitting with the right hand through the hitting zone will not overpower the left when the swing itself is sound. Centrifugal force uncocks the wrists which is a greater force than the hitting action at impact. Setting out to hit the ball simply squares the clubface at impact and adds more power by augmenting clubhead speed.

D: Helps "stay behind" and "swing through" the ball with good hand action: Three terms used in golf refer to actions that occur together and when coordinated, result in accuracy at impact: "staying behind the ball," "swinging through the ball," and "releasing the hands" through the hitting zone. Although the actions occur naturally as a result of accuracy through the swing, coordination is easier once the terms are understood.

On the downswing and through the ball, "staying behind the ball" refers to keeping the head and shoulders behind the ball by keeping the head down behind the ball as the right shoulder pulls down and under the chin. "Swinging through the ball" refers to the arms and clubhead pulling down from the top and through the ball by swinging the legs back to the left and turning the hips back through the hitting zone. Centrifugal force "releases" the hands, however, as a result of the other actions. Although the hands "release" naturally, setting out to hit the ball and completing the shoulder turn coordinates actions through the hitting zone and "releases" the hands more accurately by pulling the right shoulder downward and "squaring" the shoulders into the hitting zone.

Although the shoulders turn around the head and under the chin on both the backswing and follow-through, the shoulders arrive at impact "square and canted" just as at address. "Staying behind" and "swinging through" the ball is then a matter of keeping the head down at impact and hitting into the follow-through. Through the backswing, however, unless a hitting action and a full shoulder turn has positioned the right shoulder back to pull *downward*, the right shoulder "dives" forward from the top of the swing. When this occurs accuracy through the ball is

"Staying behind" and "swinging through the ball".

difficult because the right shoulder "comes over the top" *before* impact and pushes the head up.

Every position and movement from the start of the swing is directed toward the critical moment of impact where "staying behind the ball keeps the head behind the ball as the lower body "swings through" the hitting zone with the hands ahead of the ball. Misunderstanding the terms, however, often results in the head *and* the hands either staying behind or swinging through the ball together. For instance, even the smallest effort made toward staying completely behind the ball prevents the weight from shifting left and expends power before reaching the ball by keeping the hands behind the ball and "releasing" the hands too soon. On the other hand, letting the upper body swing back through the ball along with lower body action pulls the shoulders laterally, pulling the head beyond the ball. Although the hands pull through the ball as the weight shifts left, hitting power is diminished as the hands "release" too late.

Sliding or swaying back through the ball with the head and shoulders returns the clubface closed or "hooded" and causes various problems. "Skying" the tee shot, for instance, is a direct result of the lateral movement when combined with "picking up the clubhead" and chopping back at the ball. The sharp descent of the clubhead with a

Swaying through the ball pulls the head and shoulders beyond the ball at impact.

hooded clubface sliding under the ball hits the bottom of the ball with the top of the clubhead, accounting for the white ball marks on top of the driver. Pulling, hooking, "punching," or "smothering" the ball occurs with the other clubs as a result of the closed or hooded clubface.

Forcing the right shoulder down and under rather than using fundamental actions is a common mistake of even knowledgeable golfers because it overturns the shoulders at the top of the swing and prevents smooth coordination. It is far better—and easier—to firm the left arm, use a hitting action, and complete the shoulder turn. The action brings the right shoulder down and under naturally as the weight shifts left.

E: Stresses importance of accurate grip: Unintentional slicing, pushing, hooking, and pulling are the nemesis of every golfer. They occur less frequently among proficient golfers, but are all too often accepted as a necessary though frustrating "part of the game" by less experienced golfers. Since consistent accuracy is generally the result of many years of effort directed toward that end, these particular shots should be accepted in part by average golfers—but never as chronic problems.

Unlike poor swing movements or incorrect positions which may return the clubface square but still mis-hits the ball by not returning the clubhead accurately, the aforementioned difficulties, in particular, occur when the clubhead returns accurately but with the clubface open or closed. When that happens, an incorrect grip at address has usually precluded the ability of the hands to square the clubface at impact, especially with right hand involvement. In order to be able to hit with the right hand and square the clubface at impact, an accurate grip and square clubface *must* be established at address.

An accurate grip and square clubface at address align the back of the left hand, palm of the right hand, and the clubface directly toward the target. At impact, "natural" hand action will return the hands and clubface to these square positions when the right hand hits the ball.

With the clubface squared to the line of flight, incorrectly positioning the hands (or just one hand for that matter) too far right or too far left opens or closes the clubface at impact because a natural hitting action will return the *hands* square and turn the clubface at impact. An incorrect grip can quickly be determined at address by squaring the clubface, assuming the grip, then turning the hands into the position they return to at impact; in other words, turning the back of the left hand and palm of the right hand directly toward the target. An incorrect grip will instantly open or close the clubface at address, which is exactly what happens at impact in a natural hitting action.

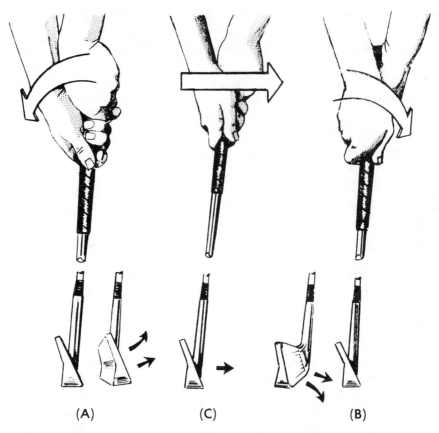

(A)   (C)   (B)

An incorrect grip can be determined at address by squaring the clubface, completing the grip, then turning the hands into the position they return to at impact. Positioning the hands too far right will close the clubface (A) and positioning the hands too far left will open the clubface (B). An accurate grip, however keeps the clubface square (C).

Although intentionally hooking or slicing can be negotiated by changing only the grip, these controlled shots are also accompanied by an open or closed stance as well as hitting on or across the line of flight. Since hooking and slicing are determined by both the angle of the clubface and the path of the clubhead through the ball, the average golfer should continue to establish square positions until the clubhead can be returned with accuracy. Returning the clubface square minimizes inaccuracy at impact when the clubhead is not hitting through the ball on the line of flight (at which time an open or closed clubface only magnifies the inaccuracy).

Studying the following diagrams will help understand the influence of an open or closed clubface at impact caused by squaring the clubface at address but positioning the hands either too far right or too far left:

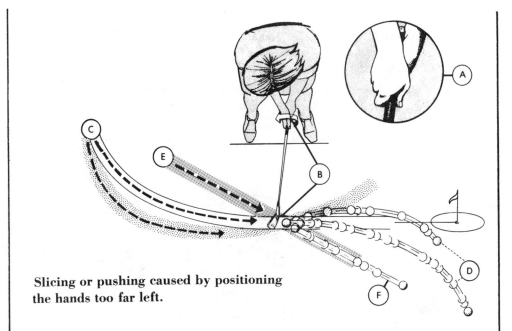

**Slicing or pushing caused by positioning
the hands too far left.**

(A) With the clubface square but the hands too far left at address. . .
(B) The hands return to "square" at impact and open the clubface.
(C) If the clubhead returns either on or from outside the line of flight. . .
(D) The open clubface cuts across the ball to slice.
(E) If the clubhead hits out across the line of flight. . .
(F) The clubface hits square and pushes the ball to the right.

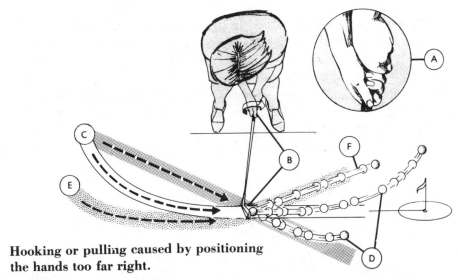

**Hooking or pulling caused by positioning
the hands too far right.**

(A) With the clubface square but the hands positioned too far right at
      address. . .

(B)   The hands return to "square" at impact and close the clubface.
(C)   If the clubhead returns either on or from inside the line of flight. . .
(D)   The closed clubface cuts across the ball to hook.
(E)   If the clubhead returns from outside the line of flight. . .
(F)   The clubface hits square and pulls the ball to the left.

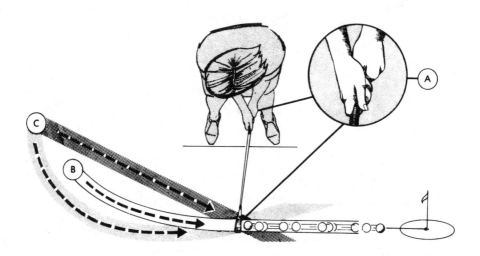

Accuracy at impact with accurate grip at address.

(A)   When the back of the left hand, palm of the right hand, and the clubface are "square" at address, they return square at impact.
(B)   Consequently. . .when the clubhead returns *on* the line of flight the clubface hits the ball straight.
(C)   Although an incorrect swing pattern which hits across the line of flight may hit the ball off-line, inaccuracy will not be magnified by an open or closed clubface.

22

Starting the Downswing

Every position and movement from the start of the swing is designed to build up power through the backswing and release it through the hitting zone by leading the downswing with the legs and hips. Data fed into the mental computer *before the backswing starts*, however, determine the start of the downswing. The movement is "programmed" from the moment the clubhead is positioned behind the ball.

Starting the downswing with lower body action delivers power at impact by shifting the weight to the left, pulling the arms down from the top, turning the hips through the ball, and releasing the hands through the hitting zone. Swinging the club back with upper body action keeps the weight on the right, expending power before reaching the hitting zone by throwing the arms and clubhead upward from the top of the swing and releasing the hands too soon.

Downswing action is a reflex action—a "moment of truth," so to speak, when positions at address and movements through the backswing prove to be right or wrong as indicated by how the downswing starts, because the downswing starts with *either* the upper or lower body as a result of what precedes the action. Although it is important to understand the reflexive downswing movement, one of the intrinsic values of understanding the overall swing is in also knowing that the reflex movement is an action that starts from the *beginning* of the swing rather than by conscious thought or action from the *top* of the swing.

Mistakes quickly show up through the backswing and are indicated by an inability of the legs and hips to start the downswing. The smallest correction before the backswing starts may correct the entire golf swing by promoting reflex action of the lower body the moment the backswing starts.

The initial movement of the legs and hips shifting the weight and pulling the arms, hands, and clubhead down from the top is so important at impact that there has been a continuing search down through the years for one "key move" to promote this downswing action. Even instructional golf continues to promote the endless search by inadvertently using terms that advocate various moves from the top of the swing to start the downswing action, such as:

Start the hips back toward the target.
Turn the hips to the left.
Start the hips back before completing the backswing.
Start the left hip back.
Start the right hip back in a "cross-lateral" shift.
"Pause" at the top to start the hips back first.
Wait for the clubhead.
Leave the clubhead at the top when the downswing starts.
Let the hips pull the arms down.
Pull the arms down from the top.
Pull the left arm down as if pulling on a bell cord.
Pull down with the three fingers of the left hand.
Pull down with the *two* fingers of the left hand.
Push off against the right foot.
Shift the weight.
Keep the head behind the ball.
Stay behind the ball.
Keep the *shoulders* behind the ball.
Swing through the ball.
Bring the right shoulder under.
Swing the legs toward the target.
Swing the *knees* toward the target.
Start the left knee toward the target.
Start the right knee toward the target.
Drive the knees toward the target.
Start the right elbow toward the left knee.
. . .etc., etc., etc.,. . .and all from the top of the swing.

Although each of the above "solutions" is occasionally used effectively (and many contribute good swing thoughts), the list makes three salient points. First, in fulfilling an obligation to students, instructional golf generally comes up with something to make the downswing work. By continuing to focus attention on action from the top, however, instructional golf must assume responsibility for poor golf instruction by creating a universal tendency to make the downswing start from the top rather than from the beginning of the swing. Second, all of the various actions should occur, and do occur, when the swing is sound. Third, almost any swing thought will start good lower body action but only when rhythm, timing, and accuracy of other positions at the top of the swing make coordination possible when the swing thought is applied.

Although any key thought may be used effectively to start the downswing, the point being missed in golf—and the most important point—is that whatever happens at the top of the swing must be the result of a key swing thought at the beginning of the swing, because starting the downswing from the top of the swing changes timing and rhythm. As important as positions and movements are in promoting reflex action, positions must still have time to coordinate and when the backswing is sound, rhythm and timing become the primary factors in moving the lower body first in the downswing action.

The advantages of a well-grooved, well-timed swing that uses "personalized" swing thoughts were discussed in Chapter 15. They are important to the swing and may be applied to anything specific that promotes a good golf swing. They can also be used to initiate the downswing. How and where these thoughts are applied, however, has great impact on the swing by influencing timing and rhythm. A change in timing or rhythm at the top of the swing caused by sudden swing thoughts either prevents reflex action from moving the lower body first or causes lower body action to react adversely by moving too quickly or moving to the right.

Golfers who have "stubbed" the clubhead going back and have experienced the difficulty in stopping the swing for "overs" have experienced the dogged determination of reflex action to finish the swing by the quick return of the clubhead. As quick and persistent as reflex action is in the downswing movement, however, the application of any swing thought at the *top* of the swing is faster—and much too fast to coordinate with a rhythmical swinging movement. The quick response of muscles to thoughts or actions at the top of the swing, moving faster than reflex action, changes timing and rhythm and moves the upper body *first*, pointing out the importance of a downswing plan *before* the backswing starts. If one move should be found to start the lower body first, it must be the key swing thought in mind before the backswing starts to maintain rhythm and timing in the reflex movement.

When positions are correct and the backswing is sound, almost any swing thought from the start of the swing may help or improve the downswing, but few work effectively from the top. The key to using a key swing thought to start an action from the top is to think of the downswing action during the waggle and maintain that thought through the backswing.

Any key thought used to "trigger" the downswing applied before the backswing starts alerts certain positions at address to prepare for coordination with the downswing action. In turn, positions involved affect backswing movements which react accordingly. For instance: if pushing off against the inside of the right foot is a conscious action found to "trigger" lower body action, thinking about the pushing action before the backswing starts, while "waggling" into the setup, alerts and reinforces the right foot and the knee for the downswing action by subconsciously positioning them for the action at address. The preplanned pushing action then keeps the weight inside the right foot through the backswing, maintaining timing and rhythm at the top of the swing by promoting the action continuously from the start of the swing. This same conscious thought at the *top* of the swing, however, kicks the whole swing out of phase, changing timing and rhythm with a sudden burst of power from the right foot. Unless the right foot and knee are prepared for the action at the start of the swing, the weight may move across the right foot on the backswing. When that occurs, any attempt to push against the foot pushes against the *outside* of the foot, rather dramatically flinging the golfer straight backward off his feet to combine with a wild flailing of the arms down first.

Sudden "slumps" in the game—when the swing gets worse for no reason—are seldom caused by knowing too much or thinking too much, but by knowing too little and *doing* the thinking right at the top of the swing. The more effort applied the worse rhythm becomes until the swing gets progressively worse. When this occurs, rhythm should be reinstated with a rhythmical waggle and "solutions" applied at the start of the swing.

Although one of the more important movements in golf, an accurate downswing is also the most commonly difficult—to the point where golfers should *search* for key swing thoughts to help improve the downswing action. Individual swings are so unique in their own weaknesses and strengths, however, and so many things affect the swing, that golfers must find thoughts of their own to fit their own golf swing. They are not the same for every golfer, nor are they consistently the same for every golfer all the time, which is part of the challenge of golf. Great golfers, however, are separated from mediocre golfers just by an ability to do such basic things as finding useful swing thoughts and knowing how and where to use them.

23

Practicing the Short Swing

Practicing the short swing described in Chapter 19 conditions the mind, as well as the muscles, and develops confidence in letting the hips and legs motivate the movement of the arms on the downswing. All of the "tools" of a full golf swing are available to work with and are used in the shorter swing: the grip, position of address, waggle, forward press, toe-up positions of the clubhead, wrist break, and hitting with the right hand. None of these must be overemphasized or allowed to overshadow the others in order to develop natural movements. Along with positions and movements, the short swing teaches balance, timing, and rhythm as keynotes of coordination.

Practicing the short swing should be used when learning, analyzing, or correcting the swing. When learning golf, fundamental positions, rhythm, and coordination are more readily developed in a smaller, controlled swing area which is not as demanding as the full golf swing. When analyzing or correcting the swing, using a shorter swing makes it easier to "sense and feel" fundamentals, to check suspected trouble areas, and to minimize thought applied to full swing action while "grooving" corrected fundamentals. In any instance, the short swing should be practiced by methodically applying fundamentals in sequence with continuous movement, checking positions for accuracy along with building up swing action.

Learning golf and practicing the short swing is similar in principle to learning to drive a car; basic learning techniques are used to slowly develop feeling and skill. It would, obviously, be foolhardy when first learning to drive to get in the car, switch on the ignition, and accelerate to a high rate of speed with no driving skills. Yet this is exactly how many golf swings evolve. In order to handle a car at a high rate of speed with natural reflexes and competency, drivers must first learn basic driving techniques, then develop these skills at the lower speeds. Such is the case with the golf swing.

Just as in learning to drive a car, proficiency and confidence develop by gradually developing skills to attain a higher level of control. Just as the short swing through the wrist break develops feeling for the full golf swing, an even smaller swing without the wrist break develops feeling for the downswing action. Keeping the hands below hip level strengthens the grip and develops feeling in the hands while developing feeling for how the legs swing naturally as the lower body responds to reflex action. It is an excellent exercise to practice.

When fundamentals are applied with deliberate accuracy, rhythm in a smaller movement combines with a firm grip and a little right-hand hitting action to set up a swinging movement of the legs, starting the lower body back as the initial forward movement and pulling the arms and hands back through the swing. The same pause felt at the top of a full golf swing (which represents good timing) occurs in the miniature short swing as coordination combines with a slow backswing to delay hand action until the hands are pulled back to the hitting zone as the weight shifts left.

The miniature movement of the short swing should be practiced until the reflex movement of the lower body is deeply ingrained by feeling. At that time the swing should gradually be lengthened, as long as the feeling is retained. At any point where reflex action leaves the swing or the action is forced to work, the procedure should be started again to regain the reflex feeling.

An accurate grip and "setup" are of particular importance when practicing any part of the swing. The smallest, most insignificant positions within these larger units may independently play predominantly important roles by promoting coordination. Nothing should be overlooked as a contributory influence on the ultimate result.

Although a precisely accurate grip can be established and checked at address, it is also reflected in an ability to hit consistently accurate shots. (Accuracy should always be an integral part of any practice session as further indication that the grip is correct.) Much can be accomplished, however, by practicing without hitting balls to focus attention on reflexive downswing action.

Part 5
The Completion of the Swing

24

Fundamental #15—The Follow-Through

Once the hands are through the hitting zone the tendency is to let momentum complete the swing, relegating the follow-through to an incidental result rather than a contributing force in the swing. It is a mistake, however, to feel that nothing can be accomplished after the ball is hit to still promote the shot. In order to complete the shot with any degree of accurate finesse, following through to the top of the swing must be regarded and practiced as an essential part of the whole.

How to Achieve Fundamental #15:

Extend the short swing into a completion of the swing by letting the hands swing on into a finished position. Let the weight shift entirely to the left side, rolling on across the left foot, and let the body turn by turning the midsection squarely toward (or even left of) the target. Let the right foot come up on the toe and hold the balanced position.

A full follow-through turns the mid-section directly toward the target.

Purposes:

A. Prevents a "lifting" left elbow.
B. Prevents "quitting on the shot."
C. Develops feeling for a completed follow-through.
D. Teaches balance.
E. Continues accelerating the clubhead through the ball.

A: Prevents a "lifting" left elbow: Just as the right elbow has a tendency to "fly" upward through the backswing and keep the clubface closed (Fundamental #10D), the left elbow may bow outward and lift upward into the follow-through and keep the clubface open. Unless the elbows point down at address and through the swing it is difficult for natural hand action to square the clubface at impact.

A lifting left elbow into the follow-through also lifts at impact, frequently "punching" the ball far right of the target line with a bowed left arm and slightly open clubface through the hitting zone. Although the elbows move away from the body to prevent restricting the swing, for accuracy through the swing and a square clubface both elbows must point down toward the ground through the golf swing.

A simple correction for "flying" elbows—either right *or* left—is to position the elbows together by rolling the elbows inward and swing with the elbows together to a completion of the swing. It must be remembered, however, that overestablishing or overcorrecting positions, in this case keeping the elbows in too tightly, causes restrictions in the swing. The arms swing *away* from the body with the elbows down for a full golf swing.

B: Prevents "quitting on the shot": Following through completely is, ideally, simply the easy result of a well-executed swing. So much emphasis is placed on just hitting the ball, however, that once the ball is on its way, very few golfers make a concentrated effort toward really finishing the shot. Consequently, most golfers are "quitting on the shot" before the swing is finished.

Although following through is not always what golfers do but what they are able to do with accuracy through the swing, it must not be completely downgraded to *only* the result of a well-executed swing. Making certain the body completes the turn by practicing following through has a tendency to correct small mistakes made through the swing by pulling the swing together. This prevents such things as getting stuck on the right side and not shifting the weight by keeping the body turning and pulling the weight to the left.

C: Develops feeling for a completed follow-through: Few golfers know what it feels like to really finish the swing in a balanced position because they have never been in that position, either accidentally or deliberately. Muscles are very reluctant to go where they have never been before and they must frequently be taught the feeling of coordination when the hands swing on to the top.

If difficulty is experienced in getting the "feel" of a full follow-through it is sometimes helpful in practice to pull the upper body away from the ball on the downswing as the weight shifts to the left. This turns the body toward the target in a reverse "C" position with the small of the back in the center of the "C." Although the movement exaggerates the action and it is not a good *swing* thought, it does develop a feeling for completing the follow-through while "staying behind" and "swinging through the ball" in a balanced position. Letting the right knee turn toward the target as the weight rolls across the left foot helps swing into the position.

Swinging into a "reverse C" position develops feeling for a full follow-through.

D: Teaches balance: Golfers unaccustomed to finishing the swing and maintaining balance may find it difficult at first to swing onto the left foot and up on the right toes, but it is helpful to understand that being up on the right toes is a fundamental position that maintains balance. Consistently falling away from the ball or staying "stuck" on the right is often overcome simply by practicing swinging into the follow-through—up on the toes—and holding the position at the top of the swing.

Balance through the swing, which helps follow through, is determined at address by establishing an upright stance while "sitting down" to the ball with the seat stuck out and keeping the weight off the toes. As mentioned before, the feeling for a balanced setup is similar in feeling to a boxer's stance, which puts strength in the legs and feeling in the feet. Practicing good balance at address and in the follow-through helps maintain balance while swinging.

E: Continues accelerating the clubhead through the ball: Finishing the shot by intentionally following through continues accelerating the clubhead through the ball with maximum clubhead speed. If golfers are unable to follow through to completely finish the swing, power is being lost at impact.

HITTING INTO THE FOLLOW-THROUGH

Hitting with the right hand.

The "toe-up" position of the clubhead in the follow-through.

The follow-through.

25

Developing the "Natural" Swing

The final stage in building the swing is an important addition to the golf swing as a whole because it deals more with the mental, rather than the physical, aspect of the game. Throughout the book, fundamentals have been presented one by one for the purpose of learning. In the process of learning, however, many mental "specifics" have been created which, if emphasized independently or taken out of context, instigate conscious thought. Although necessary at address or when studying or practicing the swing, conscious thought must not be allowed to interfere with a natural swinging action. Just as a circle is a single line, the swing is a continuous movement. And above all else, the swing *must* be a swing.

A sudden swing thought or changing the swing plan after the backswing starts is an ever-present obstacle to be overcome in golf because it changes timing in the swing and interferes with a swinging pendulum action. Although fundamentals have been presented separately, *every* fundamental has been presented in a sequence which, when connected, makes a circle in a natural swinging movement. Fundamentals will produce a sound and natural swing, just by being connected, when golfers resist the urge to make specific fundamentals work.

Golf is a unique mental and physical endeavor. Teaching a natural swing based on fundamentals and understanding *without* promoting conscious thought is an instructional challenge superseded only by the physical challenge of playing the game. In order to help develop a natural, thought-free swing, it becomes oddly necessary to conclude instruction by helping golfers learn how not to consciously apply the very things being taught.

Developing a "natural" golf swing continues to be a matter of understanding and in this instance, learning to apply fundamentals without conscious thought by understanding the following:

(A) What makes the golf swing natural.
(B) What prevents a natural swing.
(C) How to avoid conscious thought.
(D) How to apply fundamental knowledge.
(E) Practice methods that develop a natural swing.

(A) What makes the golf swing natural: Although some individuals are born with superb muscular coordination (which makes learning and playing golf less complicated), few are born with a natural golf swing. The golf swing must generally be taught or developed and evolves in four different ways: (1) by competent instruction; (2) emulation, which is imitation in order to equal or excel; (3) written instruction; and (4) personal desire and dedication. Depending upon the intensity of the latter, any or all of the four may be directed toward developing a natural, effective swing.

The first type of "natural" swing is taught by teaching swing technique based on applying fundamentals. An instructor's knowledge of fundamentals, however, may not convey understanding by explaining how these fundamentals affect the golf swing. Although this has the distinct advantage of producing a golf swing unencumbered by conscious thought, learning only swing technique leaves a golfer with an inability to analyze and correct the swing because the basic concepts, i.e., fundamentals, are not completely understood.

The difficulty with not understanding the swing is that when problems do occur—and they will—golfers eventually resort to applying swing "specifics" derived from any number of available sources, particularly written instruction and helpful fellow golfers. At this point, however, "a little bit of knowledge" becomes "a dangerous thing" in golf because it permits an application of only some fundamentals and the exclusion of others. Among those others may be the very one which prevents coordination.

Incorrectly or independently applied fundamentals not only break the circle in a continuous swinging movement, but change the pattern of the swing. Conscious thought, which is so destructive to the swinging movement, then slowly creeps into a swing which is neither fundamentally sound nor understood. This happens because attention is focused on forcing the swing to work by emphasizing positions or movements which *are* understood in an ineffectual effort toward compensating for missing fundamentals. Since the solution rarely relates to the problem, this further disturbs the original "natural" swing and a bad situation gets progressively worse. Compensating for missing fundamentals, even as a temporary measure, is an ill-advised method for rectifying problems because it grooves imperfections into the swing, which then requires further compensation. Unless the basic difficulty is corrected by accurate self-analysis or professional help, enter despair and frustration!

When the swing is sound and positions known to be correct, conscious thought can readily be transformed into concentration to restore the natural swing. There should be an obligation on the part of instructors to teach understanding along with swing technique so golfers will be able to correct and keep the swing intact in order to play consistent, if not spectacular, golf.

The second type of "natural" swing can be developed by emulation. With a personal desire to equal or excel, young people in particular, who are great imitators, have become exceptionally competent golfers as a result of imitation. Cases in point are young caddies of yesteryear emulating great golfers of their time, or children in golfing families. And today, of course, with touring professionals, golf clinics, television, and excellent book and magazine illustrations made using high-speed photography, there is the added advantage of being able to study the swing very closely. Although a natural swing can be developed by this kind of study and observation (without knowing *how* the golf swing works) there are disadvantages to learning only by emulation. A poor golf swing can be copied as well as a good golf swing and without understanding how the golf swing works, it is unlikely that all of the fundamentals will be incorporated into the swing to develop either a sound technique or total potential—which includes an ability to find and correct swing defects.

The third type of "natural" swing can be developed by studying and applying written instruction, but not all written instruction includes all of the fundamentals that establish positions which promote coordination—which is the purpose of building the swing. The advantage of developing a natural swing based upon written instruction is in learning to apply fundamentals which make the golf swing natural while at the same time learning what *prevents* the swing from working.

The drawback to developing a swing based solely on written instruction is that golf instruction continues to promote a belief that teaching golfers more than what are referred to as "basic fundamentals" creates a tendency toward making the golf swing work by playing analytical golf. Consequently, both written and professional instruction generally teach fundamentals only through the position of address but are then more apt to stress swing technique without teaching additional fundamentals. Although the instruction is accurate and continues to relate to the basic swing, total effectiveness is still dependent upon correct positions and movements throughout the swing. Most written instruction seldom includes enough fundamental instruction for golfers to develop a completely natural swing by teaching fundamentals on through to a completion of the swing. It is difficult to develop or correct the swing, however, without guidelines and checkpoints beyond the position of address.

The fourth method of developing a "natural" swing—personal desire—is the very foundation for learning the age-old game. Any form of instruction is effective with enthusiasm for playing but personal desire alone will not develop a golf swing. The swing is too complex. A desire to learn the game combined with competent instruction that teaches understanding as well as swing technique provides an opportunity to study, observe, and apply any instruction effectively.

(B) What prevents a "natural" swing: Former great golfer Walter Hagen once responded to the statement, "You have to be dumb to play that game" with the comment, "You don't have to be, but it helps," pointing out the desirable, although somewhat unrealistic, advantage of just having a natural swing. Such a comment indicates that accomplished golfers do recognize conscious thought as a threat to a natural swinging movement, but the swing capability of a really accomplished golfer also indicates that fundamentals are understood and applied and that conscious thought can be overcome—first by application of conscious thought, then by practice to turn it into concentration.

Golfers are kept off-balance and somewhat confused by being told on the one hand to just have a natural swing by thinking of nothing but swinging, while at the same time being presented annually with reams of printed *specific* instruction with encouragement to apply it in the swing. Unless the swing is particularly sound and fundamentally strong, however, this type of instruction encourages conscious thought by presenting fundamentals out of context. It is senseless, for instance, to instruct a golfer (or for a golfer to instruct himself) that keeping the left arm straight will correct a faulty swing if the hips are open at address or the grip incorrect.

Golf instruction remains in the dark ages of instructional technique at times and frequently displays great inconsistency in not deciding what or how much golfers *should* know to develop a natural swing. In a misdirected effort toward avoiding conscious thought, both teachers and students inadvertently steer away from the very thing which is needed to prevent mental interference, which is total understanding and application of all of the fundamentals necessary to create a natural swing. Bits and pieces of golf instruction can only be applied to a swing which is fundamentally sound to begin with, whereupon the swing gets progressively better.

Part of the difficulty in developing a natural swing stems from the very thing which appears to make golf easy: the ball is a stationary target. Unlike other sports such as tennis, baseball, volleyball, soccer, table tennis, etc., where the ball "in play" is a moving target, a golf ball sits motionless on the tee or ground. Rather than simplifying things, however, this complicates the game because the time allowed in getting *ready* to hit a stationary target, particulary with the "playing field" interspersed with bunkers, barrancas, trees, and lakes, also allows time for the mind to become involved and overcome the natural reflex action of hitting a moving target.

Although returning a moving ball requires specific skills which relate to the individual sport, the reflex action involved allows limited time to become involved with such things as positions or movements, swing technique, or losing points *or* the ball in a hazard. Lacking time for apprehension (tension) to restrict the swing, a moving ball is returned with a looser, reflexive response. With unlimited time allowed for setting up to the ball in golf, however, there is also time to become too mentally involved—particularly when confronted with making a fairly difficult golf shot. It is difficult to make golf shots when the mind interferes with a natural swinging movement.

Overcoming the mental obstacle of hitting a stationary target is partly a matter of trusting fundamentals, practicing setting up more quickly, then swinging. With practice, this develops the same reflex action involved in hitting a moving target by starting a rhythmical swinging movement from the moment the clubhead is soled behind the ball.

(C) How to avoid conscious thought: Aside from the above, there are only two ways to develop the same uncomplicated reflex swinging movement used in hitting a moving object to hit a stationary golf ball, thereby avoiding conscious thought: either a golfer must just have a natural swing and be a confident golfer who applies fundamentals without any complication derived from having to understand them, or else develop a natural swing based on complete understanding of all of the fundamentals, then overcome conscious thought by application and practice. The irony of golf, however, is there *is* no "in between"! Very few golfers know either nothing *or* everything about the golf swing, and the little bit of knowledge that every golfer has is the very thing which causes conscious thought and prevents a natural swing.

Since it is unlikely in this highly instructed game that golfers are able to remain uninformed, know nothing about the swing, and apply only a thought-free workable swing technique, it is sensible to presume that expanding on knowledge will help develop actions that make the golf swing natural. Developing a natural swing, however, is not only a matter of understanding the swing and trusting fundamentals, but accepting certain facts:

(1) Dedicated golfers *cannot* know too much about the swing. The single fundamental which is missing from the swing may be the very one that prevents coordination. Knowing too little about the swing causes conscious thought by creating a tendency toward applying mental "specifics" to compensate for missing fundamentals.

(2) Correctly applied fundamentals will produce a natural swing when they are all connected by a rhythmically smooth and continuous swinging movement by putting the swing in motion from the moment the clubhead is soled behind the ball.

(3) When all of the fundamentals are applied correctly, rhythm and timing promote coordination and are keynotes in a reflex swinging movement.

(4) Analysis and corrections should be made only when chronic difficulty occurs. Many things affect the swing and everyone hooks and slices and mis-hits the ball. The object is to smooth the swing so consistency develops by missing fewer shots.

(5) When chronic difficulty does occur, rebuild the swing in practice and check every fundamental. Use the short swing and slow down rhythm to correct positions and movements.

(6) Fear of "making the shot" or taking too long to set up to the ball creates tension which prevents swinging rhythmically with a reflex movement. Trust fundamentals, practice setting up quickly, and use the same golf swing for each golf shot.

(7) Concentration and confidence replace conscious thought and indecision by practicing the waggle—and nothing suffices like practice to develop a natural swing. Confidence, as well as the swing, can be grooved in practice by applying fundamentals directed toward a reflexive swing technique. Confidence developed in practice is an integral part of golf.

(D) How to apply fundamental knowledge: "Purposes" defined throughout the book help understand the swing. They play no part in applying fundamentals. A natural swing develops by putting into effect only "how to achieve" the fundamentals, and "purposes" attained are gratifying results of correctly applied fundamentals. The following few pages present a quick review of fundamentals, highlighting the essential requirements for developing a natural swing.

Assume the left hand grip. Using only the left hand, comfortably extend the left arm so the arm and shaft are in a straight line with each other and square the clubface to the target. Stand upright with the feet together and square the feet to the square clubface.

Move first the left foot, then the right to the width of the shoulders, squaring the feet to the line of flight. Angle the left foot slightly open in relationship to the slightly closed right foot.

"Sit" straight down to the ball by flexing the knees slightly inward and stick the seat out a bit. Let the left hand move slightly down and inward.

Complete the grip by loosely placing the right hand on the club, making certain to retain the square position of the hips. At this point, the stance is upright, bent slightly from the waist with the weight toward the heels and on the inside of the feet. The right shoulder is lower than the left, but the entire position of address is "square."

Although conscious thought is necessary to establish the position of address, "sense and feel" take over as each specific position is waggled into an interlocked relationship with each other by an up and down movement of the body and the clubhead. As the waggle coordinates positions, conscious thought changes into concentration by a slight back and forth movement of the clubhead behind the ball as a deliberate swing plan is put into effect. Positions are secured by rolling the elbows toward each other, firming the left arm, but positioning the looser right arm slightly lower than the left. Firming the grip and pressing the right hand down and forward, rock the legs slightly forward to start the movement of the swing.

The backswing starts with the forward movement, whereupon the firm, extended left arm pushes the clubhead away from the ball and into and through the toe-up position in the background. At this point, a well-disciplined swing developed through understanding and practice keeps the right elbow down and the left knee pointing forward. Setting out to hit the ball combines a swinging movement with a hitting action to start a coordinated, powerful swing.

As the clubhead is pushed on through to a completion of the backswing, the shoulders turn the hips. The shoulder turn and pivot are natural results of pushing the clubhead back, rocking the weight to the right and turning against the braced right foot with the knee inside the right instep. Keeping the left knee pointing ahead as the leg swings inward puts the "swing" in golf while building body torque.

A good swing thought at the beginning of the swing results in reflex movement at the top of the swing. Rhythm and timing create a tiny pause at the top of the backswing as the backswing transfers to the downswing. Reflex action starts the hips back first with swinging leg action, shifting the weight back to the left and pulling the arms down from the top.

Hitting through the ball with the right hand is an intentional action from the start of the swing that squares the clubface at impact and extends the right arm through the ball, whereupon keeping the head down and hitting into the toe-up position on the directional line keeps the hands hitting toward the target as the hips turn through the ball. As the weight shifts on across the left foot, the right foot comes up on the toe and the body turns squarely toward the target in a balanced, completed swing.

(E) Practice methods to develop a natural swing: Relatively few golfers, even though dedicated to self-improvement, really know how or what to practice without professional help. Consequently, observing golfers on a driving range frequently resembles a paid admission spectator sport, often giving the impression that while practicing imperfection, the object of hitting balls is to get rid of them as fast and as far as possible with maximum muscular intent. Understanding the swing, however, or having professional guidance, provides specific objectives for productive practice sessions.

Although effort should always be directed toward developing a natural, thought-free swing, practicing is where thinking should be done. Practicing is more of a mental game complicated by physical involvement rather than a physical game complicated by mental involvement, which is apt to be true when playing golf.

Practicing should be determined by personal capability, progress, and various needs of individuals from beginning to professional golfers and should not be based upon a sudden desire to attain the unattainable or just *be* an accomplished golfer. A student golfer, for instance, is ill equipped to practice the finer technique of an expert and should practice swing "specifics" until the swing is fundamentally sound.

A countless number of things can be practiced, but there are certain procedures which should be followed in every practice session:

(1) Knowing *what* to practice is the key to a successful practice session. Have a positive thought in mind regarding what is to be accomplished. Unless something is radically wrong, practicing only rhythm, timing, and hitting the ball helps groove smooth consistency.

(2) General practice should start by "smoothing" the swing with soft nine-iron shots, working up through the clubs to the driver. Maximum power should only be added when the swing is rhythmically smooth.

(3) Rhythm and timing, which promote coordination, should be an integral part of each practice shot. A rhythmical count may help such as "back-and-through" or "one-and-two," pausing at the top as the downswing starts and hitting the ball on "two." The speed of the count fits rhythm to the natural tempo of each individual's swing, which may vary between fast and slow. Whatever the count or tempo may be,

however, it should remain the same for each golf shot within each individual's swing to develop consistency.

(4) Always line up on a target. Practicing distance without accuracy develops a false sense of security on the practice range which results in insecurity on the course.

(5) Although distance and direction are primary goals, take time to learn "feeling" and balance through the swing by learning to *feel* positions and movements at various points through the swing. This requires ignoring the result of the shot at times.

Developing a natural swing has been a continuing process throughout the book, with Chapter 18 on "Practicing the Backswing" in particular presenting guidelines to follow for practicing the full golf swing. Special emphasis has been placed on practicing each motion of the swing. A natural swing is obtained by swinging smoothly through these sections, using all of the fundamentals to build a sound golf swing.

Nothing is more self-satisfying than developing a natural swing and being able to keep the swing intact by adjustment or correction. It is a continually rewarding experience. The golf swing, however, is as unpredictable as the weather, capricious as the wind, and seldom permanently contained. It is not uncommon for even experienced golfers to sometimes sense the swing must have a mind of its own and a rather whimsical delight in simply using the golfer as an outlet for its own self-expression. Because of the complexity of the swing and its somewhat whimsical nature, even experienced golfers are not always able to find or correct chronic problems in golf and have long since learned that the swing cannot be forced to conform. Forcing conformity into the swing simply turns on its rebellious nature—and the more insistent the golfer, the more rebellious the swing. When chronic trouble does occur, it is truly the mark of an expert to accept limitations and learn when to call on additional, outside help.

Once the swing is developed, if problems are not resolved in practice, golfers with sound golf swings who understand the swing will profit immeasurably from even one practice session with a competent instructor. A golf swing based on fundamentals is easily corrected by an expert, if not the golfer himself. Even professionals seek professional help simply because it is far easier to see a flaw than to feel it in the swing. Average golfers, however, particularly those who have built their swings on fundamentals, should be just as selective as professionals in seeking professional help by selecting professional instructors who have also built their knowledge on the use of fundamentals.

Amy and the author are pictured discussing their own golf swings while working on *Building Your Swing for Better Golf.*

Part 6
Golf Swing Problems
and Solutions

Down through the centuries, golf has become the most personally challenging game involving the largest number of players throughout the world, partly because those who pursue the game accept the frustration as part of the challenge of playing. Because of the dedication of so many to a game that is loved so much, golf continues to command the attention of those still searching for ways to lessen the frustration and increase the pleasure of golf; many hundreds of books have been written directed toward this end. Regardless of how finely the swing is perfected, however, problems still occur in golf which, oddly enough, is part of its fascination.

Understanding the golf swing helps prevent problems in golf by learning how to improve the swing to promote more accuracy and better coordination. And knowing how to correct certain fundamentals that relate to specific golf problems helps overcome recurrent problems in golf as a result of a faulty swing. A single factor remains, however, that still makes it difficult for golfers to improve beyond understanding or improving the overall swing: most golfers are unable to determine what the *basic* problems are that cause additional problems in golf.

Golf swing problems are both obvious and underlying, but underlying problems are the basic problems in golf because obvious results are caused by small, insignificant things that are often overlooked. Slicing, for instance, is an obvious problem and is generally *caused* by obvious problems such as an incorrect grip or open stance at address. Although slicing may be the obvious result of a faulty grip or stance, however, the underlying cause may be incorrect procedures used to establish the grip or stance. Incorrect procedures used to establish positions at address is a common cause of problems. Such things are seldom corrected, however, because they are seldom recognized as underlying causes of problems.

The result of the golf swing is influenced by many things such as positions and movements, timing and rhythm, dedication and practice, and physical *and* mental ability. Considering the many factors involved that may also affect the swing adversely, it is neither realistic to presume that the same poor result of different golf swings is caused by the same imperfections nor that a problem may be corrected with a single, easy solution. Every factor involved in golf affects every swing differently and there may be one or several reasons for any poor result of any golf swing.

The following problem section is not intended to be the panacea for quick eradication of every personal problem in golf, for obviously it would not be possible to personalize the section and say, "This is your problem and this is how you correct it." Correction is still a matter of knowing what the problem is in order to be able to correct it. Although any specific problem may be caused by a number of things too numerous to mention, all golf problems have *basic* reasons for why the problem occurs—and correcting the common cause is usually sufficient to overcome any specific problem.

The problem section lists problems in golf along with common causes and corrections. The purpose of the section is twofold: to help golfers find solutions to their problems and correct them, and to familiarize golfers with what the problems are in golf along with the causes that affect their own golf swing.

Aside from the fact that correcting the swing is difficult without understanding what the problems are in golf, additional difficulty is encountered by not knowing what is *right* as well as what is wrong when looking for solutions. Checking off areas that are known to be correct is a positive approach to finding underlying causes simply by eliminating the other possible causes. Eliminating causes which do *not* relate leaves causes to consider as personal problems in golf.

Problem	*Common Causes—Understanding and Correcting*
Alignment, difficulty with	Difficulty "sighting" target line, 58(B), 70-71(C), 228(4)
	Positioning feet before squaring clubface, 57-58(A), 69-71(C)
	Positioning hands behind ball, 60-61(E)
	See also Position of address, establishing
Backswing, fast	Fast waggle and poor concentration, 109-12, 179-80
	Misunderstanding hitting action in golf, 194-95(B)
	Insufficient practice in starting deliberately slow movement, 141-42(H)
	Positioning hands to pull rather than push clubhead away from ball, 59-60(E)
incomplete	*See* Shoulder turn, incomplete or restricted; Swaying
starting, difficulty	Having no procedure to follow for setting up at address, 44-45
	Leaving out the "running start" and rocking forward movement, 119-21(C), 154-56(D)
	See also Tension
stopping, difficulty	Stubbing clubhead going back, 156-207
	Starting too fast. *See* Backswing, fast
Balance, difficulty establishing and maintaining	Stance too narrow, 75-77(E)
	Leaning over too far with weight on toes, 52-53(B), 58-59(D)
	Incorrect "sitting down" position with hips tucked under, 90-91(A)
	Swinging too fast, 141-42(H)

Heels, incorrect action of	*See* Footwork
Hips, open at address	Completing grip and positioning clubhead before "sitting down" to ball, 95-97(A)
	Not understanding that the hips may inadvertently slip open while setting up to the ball, 51-52(A)
	Angle of right foot entirely closed, 73(6)
	Pressing hands too far forward with either waggle or forward press, 118(A), 118-19(B)
Hitting behind the ball	*See* Ball, falling away from; Hands, hitting from the top
Hitting from the top	*See* Hands
Hooking	Clubhead returning either on or from inside line of flight and "cutting across" ball with clubface closed, 203-4
	Square clubface at address with either hand positioned too far right, 201-2(E)
	Any closed position established at address, 46-48
	Insufficient practice in developing short swing accuracy, 183-84, 209-10
	See also Clubhead, picking up; Elbow, "flying" right; Wrist break, incorrect
"Killing" the ball	*See* Ball
Knees, incorrect action of	Lowering body too far at address by bending knees too much, 91(A)
	Right knee "swaying" beyond right instep, 102(4)
	Insufficient practice swinging into follow-through, 215-16(C)
	Encouraging left knee to jut forward or dip downward, 135-37(E) — often as result of one of following:
	(a) Weight shifting left while setting up at address, 92-93(C)
	(b) Incorrect use of forward press, 119-21(C)

Slicing	Clubhead either (a) returning from outside line of flight with square or open clubface; or (b) returning on the line of flight with clubface open, 203; often as a result of any of following:
	Square clubface at address with either hand positioned too far left, 201-2(E)
	Any open position established at address, 46-47
	Incorrect use of waggle or forward press, 118(A), 118-19(B)
	Pulling clubhead away from ball and looping the face open, 59-60(E)
	Flat swing pattern, 147-50(B)
	Collapsed left wrist at top of swing, 165-68(7)
	Incomplete or incorrect shoulder turn, 170-71(10)
	Leaving right hand out of hitting action, 195-97(C)
	Insufficient practice in developing short-swing accuracy, 209-10
Smothered hook	Clubface closed and hooded at impact. *See* Clubface, hooded; Hooking
Smothering	Clubface square at impact but hooded. *See* Clubface, hooded
Spinning out	Turning too far too soon from top of swing, 170-71(10), 189(B)
	Angle of left foot too open, 74
	Trying to "free" the follow-through by spinning around on left heel rather than rolling across the left foot, 73-75(D). *See also* Blocking out
Stance, establishing	*See* position of address
Swaying, away from ball	Knees bent forward rather than flexed inward and/or angle of right foot open, 72-73(3), 92-93(C), 162(4), 162(5)

reverse	Weight shifting left (rather than right) as backswing starts, then shifting right (rather than left) as downswing starts: generally as result of either establishing weight on left foot and/or dipping left knee, 67-69(A), 135-37(E)
Whiffing	*See* Ball
Wrist break, incorrect	Collapsed left wrist at top of swing, 165-68(7), generally caused by any or all of following:

    (a) Left hand grip too far right, 33(D)

    (b) Using incorrect procedure to position left hand, 28-30(A), 59-61(E), 69(B)

    (c) Increased momentum at top of swing as result of swinging too fast, 141-42(H)

    (d) Incorrect positions or movements that fail to swing right palm under shaft at top of swing, 168-69(8)

    (e) Not understanding how or where the wrists should break, 146

    See also Clubhead, picking up